BICYCLING
A HISTORY

BICYCLING
A HISTORY

Frederick Alderson

PRAEGER PUBLISHERS
New York · Washington

BOOKS THAT MATTER
Published in the United States of America
in 1972 by Praeger Publishers, Inc
111 Fourth Avenue, New York, N.Y. 10003

© 1972 by Frederick Alderson

Library of Congress Catalog Card number:
72-80696

Printed in Great Britain

'A prolific and well-nigh inexhaustible subject and limited space have little affinity'

Harry Hewitt Griffin
Cycles and Cycling 1890

CONTENTS

CONTENTS

LIST OF ILLUSTRATIONS

Grateful acknowledgement is made to the undermentioned for permission to reproduce illustrations, photographic or line, on the pages indicated:

The proprietors of CYCLING, pp54, 125, 135, 159
J. M. DENT and SONS, p96
GLASGOW MUSEUM OF TRANSPORT, pp17, 18, 36, 71, 89, 107
HORSHAM MUSEUM, pp 35, 53
KEYSTONE PRESS AGENCY, pp126, 144
BRIAN LAMBIE, Esq, GLADSTONE COURT MUSEUM, BIGGAR, p72
LONGMANS, GREEN & CO, pp55, 64, 132
The proprietors of the WIGAN OBSERVER, p143
H. V. WILKINSON, Esq, Windermere, pp90, 108

Apologies are tendered for any inadvertent omission in acknowledgement.

CHAPTER ONE

FORERUNNERS:
DANDY RIDERS

THE HISTORY of wheeled vehicles originates in that region of lower Mesopotamia where the first of man's cities, temples and irrigation systems appeared. There is evidence that the Sumerians, a central Asian people who settled, about 5000 BC, in the southern part of the plain of Shinar, or Sumer—where Babylon was to rise after another three millennia—made use of such vehicles about 3500 BC. They left decipherable cuneiform writing and had also discovered the use of bronze. By such standards the history of the wheeled vehicle in the West is recent. The coach was introduced to Britain from the continent in 1551. The history of the two- or three-wheeled man-powered vehicle, in this context, goes back only to yesterday. One's grandfather may well have ridden a specimen of the second, or conceivably even of the first, form of recognisable bicycle.

The idea of man in self-propelled motion is of course considerably older than this. The mythical centaur dimly prefigures a possibility only less tantalising than that envisaged in the myth of

11

Pegasus. But while wings for man still remained illusory, wheels were waiting only for adaptation to human capabilities. Until close on the end of the eighteenth century in Britain, however, the possibility of propelling a light vehicle by human muscular effort had resulted only in designs for a cumbersome manumotive travelling chaise, with its lever planks operated by a footman behind, while the occupant in front steered by cords or reins attached to the front axle.

The centaur figure became fact when the 'Célérifère' was demonstrated by M de Sivrac, sometimes known later as Comte de Sivrac, in the gardens of the Palais Royal, Paris, 1791. Probably a development of a children's toy, in the form of a wooden horse with wheels for hooves, it consisted of a rough wooden bar supported on two sizeable wheels and carrying a padded saddle. The rider propelled it by thrusting his feet alternately against the ground and could only deviate from a straight course by leaning or banking. The same sort of vehicle, some say, had been imaginatively rendered in a stained-glass window, dated 1642, in the church of Stoke Poges, near Windsor, and derived originally from the medieval hobbyhorse. The Buckinghamshire county archivist's statement that the window appears to be of Flemish or German glass, of seventeenth- or possibly sixteenth-century origin, and that in medieval iconography the conception of cherubim and seraphim riding on a wheel was not unusual, lends ammunition to the doubters of any such hobbyhorse association with cherubim, however imaginative. (Churches at Coventry and at Cirencester also have stained-glass windows with cherubim standing upon wheels of white fire.)

The major drawback of the Célérifère, or, in English, Celeripede, was its rider's very limited control of direction, the front wheel being rigidly attached to the frame and its fork having no swivelling action. Even when renamed the 'Vélocifère', two years later, it did not overcome that disability. Its appeal as a fashionable diversion among the Incroyables during the French Directory was largely

a *succes de fou* : riders calling themselves 'Vélocipèdes' formed a
club to run races along the Champs Elysées.

> I amuse each Jack o' Dandy:
> E'en great men sometimes have me handy!
> Who, when on me they get astride
> Think that on Pegasus they ride.

In this heyday of coach travel, with the horse always in the forefront as man's normal aid to or means of locomotive progress, the
next appearance of a two-wheeled vehicle maintained the centaur
suggestion. In 1817 Karl, Baron von Drais de Sauerbrun, of Mann-
heim, added a steerable front wheel to the Vélocifère, by passing
the fork through a socket. He made use of it on his journeys as an
agriculturist and Master of the Woods and Forests to the Duke of
Baden over rough and hilly country. This improved hobbyhorse or
'dandy horse'—contemporary prints often show versions with a
small horse's head on the lateral bar supporting the padded saddle
(see plate, p17)—became more widely known as the Draisienne.
After it had appeared in public in the Luxembourg Gardens the
following spring, it came to be regarded in some degree as a means
of serious transport, rather than merely of novel pastime.

An example of the hobbyhorse, included in the Bartleet Collection of Historic Cycles, now in the Herbert Museum, Coventry, has
footrests on the frontwheel spindle for the rider's relief while
'coasting' downhill, a cantilever spring under the saddle for his
comfort, and holes in the back-wheel fork for adjusting the distance
from saddle to ground, to suit his leg reach. The first accessory—
a mileometer—was fitted to a Draisienne's rear wheel in 1825. On
such machines journeys of up to fifty miles a day could be made:
a performance of 37km in 2½hr, giving an average speed of 15kph,
is recorded. They weighed about 50lb.

Later, some French rural postmen were equipped with improved
'dandy horses' for a short period under the administration of M
Dreuze. (Later still, after the Franco-Prussian War, the French

made the discovery that the steerable Célérifère had been invented not by a German, but by one of their own countrymen, Nicéphore Niepce of Chalons, the same who in 1816 made an 'artificial eye' from a small box with a lenticular glass and so won official recognition as the inventor of camera photography. He was said to have added steering to an improved Célérifère produced by him in the same year.)

Crude as the Draisienne now appears it enjoyed widespread popularity among the wealthy in Germany, Great Britain and the USA where a patent was granted, in June 1819, to W. K. Clarkson for an 'improvement in Velocipedes'. Perched on a saddle cushion in the middle of a longitudinal bar, over two equal-sized wooden wheels held in iron forks, with another cushion in front to lean upon whilst steering and propelling the machine with as forcible strides as possible, the rider cannot have been either comfortable or elegant. But the age was one in which hard exercise and spartan habits were no strangers even to the rich and noble. The London coachmaker, Denis Johnson, who copied and sold the Draisienne as a 'pedestrian curricle' at eight or ten guineas, set up a school for such riders. He turned out some hundreds of machines, including a lady's model weighing 66lb, on which after training the rider could urge himself forward 'without difficulty' at the rate of nearly ten miles an hour. Clearly it was more speedy than going any long distance on foot. Contemporary prints show also a three-wheeled type, with a lady sitting down, chairborne, on a platform over two rear wheels, while her gallant in front paddles her along.

The caricaturists, naturally, had a field day. Alken, Cruikshank, and Rowlandson depict the exertions of the Regency bucks and beaux, of the dignified and the obese—not excluding the Prince Regent—at their new riding exercise with spills and collisions galore. One drawing shows the stout prince lying lengthwise on a hobbyhorse, face downwards, holding on to the front wheel *provided with cranks* and evidently propelling the machine. Had this

14

prophetic artist applied his design practically the bicycle would have been created there and then.

Bitter satire and fierce ridicule almost killed the hobbyhorse in France. But although this 'modern Pegasus' was characterised as the perambulator by which you can ride at your ease and are obliged to walk in the mud at the same time, London so eagerly adopted what Paris was fighting shy of that John Keats could refer to the hobbyhorse as 'the "nothing" of the day'. Corinthians, amateurs of the ring and the coachman's box, paddled their mounts enthusiastically both through the parks and on the streets. In a series of twelve advertisements for a £20,000 lottery, in about 1825, one accompanies its amusing woodcut of such a rider with the following verse:

HAIRBRAIN
This is the man in an instant forsook
His home and in haste a velocipede took ;
Who through thick and thin with rapidity sped
Till his hat flying off made him light in the head ;
Yet cunningly thought he had no time to spare
As he wished to obtain Twenty Thousand, and share
In the Cash in the House that Jack built.

Some of the pedestrian hobbyhorses, as also the lady's accelerator or 'pilentum', share the attractive lines of the curricle and phaeton of the day. A Jane Austenish figure depicted riding a pilentum in the park of a country mansion maintained both grace and dignity —but here the lady's feet are not engaging the ground. A print showing a match between a top-booted rider mounted on a real horse and a rival in full riding rig on a hobbyhorse, entitled 'Match against Time or Wood beats Blood and Bone', puts the machine in its sporting context and also heralds future developments. 'Patronised by Dandies and is now expected to outrun all the First Blood in the turf!' The latter half of the statement was to come remarkably and literally true. An enterprising bootmaker even produced a special shoe, with iron-clad sole, to withstand the rider's impact on the road. Another contemporary caricature shows blacksmiths at a posting stage in angry pursuit of a hobby-rider and intent on smashing the machine—because hobbies never need to be shod.

The hobbyhorse vogue flared up among other pastimes of the urban well-to-do, such as shooting parties, steeplechases, hunting with the Old Berkeley or the Epping Hunt, fishing up river or cricketing at Lord's in top hats, and then fizzled out. But there were several attempts to effect propulsion without the direct thrust of feet on the ground. That method, after all, was too laborious, the jarring of iron-shod wheels scarcely pleasant and the rider's awkward position a possible cause of hernia. 'One might as well have walked if it had not been for the look of the thing', as the Irishman said of riding in a sedan chair with no bottom. So also in New York, where a Draisienne had been brought in 1819, ridicule and lack of real interest prevented its survival.

In that same year John Baynes, a working cutler of Leeds, worked out a scheme for operating levers and treadles to effect propulsion, but the design was too complicated—the early inventors' besetting sin—and, so far as known, without practical application. In 1819 also Edmund Cartwright DD, who had been educated at Wakefield Grammar School and was inventing to the end of a long lifetime, is credited with building a pedomotive carriage or quadricycle, propelled by pedals—one of the earliest links between 'manumotive' and cycle. He had already, after visiting Arkwright's cotton spinning mills, invented the power-loom in 1785, and within the same decade the wool-combing machine. The *Mechanics' Magazine* of the 1820s reveals that not a few other enthusiastic inventors had designs—for 'bivectors', 'trivectors', 'manuvelociters' and similar accelerators: notably Lewis Gompertz, a Surrey man, who produced in 1821 a free-wheeling machine, in which the action of pulling the steering handles caused the front wheel to turn, by means of a toothed quadrant which engaged with a pinion on the hub, and thus supplemented ordinary leg action. To give the rider

Page 17 : An early print showing hobbyhorses. Note the three-wheeled version!

Page 18 : Hobbyhorse or dandy-horse

better purchase there was a padded rest above the saddle to support his chest and shoulders. Professor Faraday is said to have built himself a velocipede of sorts and used it to ride along the corridors of the lecture theatre at the Royal Institution in 1826, as the orientalist Arthur Waley was to use a safety to do his rounds in the British Museum a century after.

But, like the hobbyhorse, these designs for mechanically propelled mounts either came to nothing more, in that age before the first wood blocks had taken the place of cobbles in Oxford Street, and when instead of Peel's 'Bobbies' with their top-hats and truncheons, sleepy turnpike men manned London Bridge, or else shortly disappeared into limbo. (The resurrected hobbyhorse, sketched in the *English Mechanic* in the sixties, advanced as it was compared to the originals, was only a rule-proving exception to this.) The age, however, remained one of belief in machinery—as the *Working Man's Companion*, 1831, sought to persuade its readers —and especially of the belief that 'all machines which facilitate the general communication between man and man, whether from town to town, from district to district, from county to county, or from nation to nation, advance the general welfare of mankind.'

B

CHAPTER TWO

BONESHAKERS

THREE LOWLAND Scots have their permanent historical niche for their major contributions towards progress in personal locomotion and in road travel—John Loudon McAdam, Kirkpatrick Macmillan and John Boyd Dunlop. McAdam, a road trustee in Ayrshire, found the existing roads 'loose, rough, perishable, expensive, tedious and dangerous to travel on'. His long course of experiments led, by 1823, to general recognition that the solution was 'macadamisation' of highways—roads constructed of small, broken stone and raised above the level of the adjoining land for drainage —and to his appointment four years later as general surveyor of roads. Macmillan, 1810-78, a blacksmith of Courthill, Dumfriesshire, devised a two-wheeled machine operated with a drive by treadles to the rear wheel and, as a tablet on the wall of his smithy recorded, so built the first pedal cycle or bicycle. The exact date, 1839 or 1840, has not been definitely established. (The claim, of course, should be noticed in passing that a Russian serf from the Urals, named Artomonov, had constructed a more advanced model forty years earlier.) Dunlop's contribution, subservient to both McAdam's and Macmillan's, was still to come.

Macmillan rode on his bicycle the fourteen miles from Courthill to Dumfries on many occasions and once, in 1842, to Glasgow. Although his machine no longer exists, the existence of the old pattern and plans of the bicycle were known to James Johnston, a member of Glasgow Cycling Club late last century. A facsimile of the machine built for him by their possessor, Thomas McCall, was sent to the Exhibition of Cycles held at the Crystal Palace, 1896, and is now on show in the Science Museum in London. Until then the belief was general that a contemporary copyist of Macmillan, Gavin Dalzell, a cooper from Lanarkshire, who came from an inventive family, had invented the bicycle. His machine, made in 1845, on which he is said to have beaten the King's Mail Coach (compelled by statute to cover ten miles within the hour) still survives. It reproduced the main features of Kirkpatrick Macmillan's treadles, with rods to cranks on the rear axle, wooden wheels with iron rims, no brakes, was accurately drawn for *Bicycle News* in 1889, and is claimed, at the Museum of Transport, Glasgow, as the oldest surviving pedal cycle in the world. It was originally thought that Dalzell had constructed and ridden a practical bicycle in 1835.

The Macmillan pedal cycle, in spite of its cranks and swinging levers, was probably set in motion by the hobbyhorse method, and its pilot wheel was steered by direct sloping forks. But it was quite different from the hobbyhorse, could be easily balanced and continuously propelled by treadle action, and had the refinement of both front and rear axle running in brass bearings. Macmillan was the first to discover that two wheels placed in line could be so balanced and propelled, without touching the ground with the feet. The machine was not patented, however, and, while it appeared on the country roads of Scotland, copied by other wheelwrights— one called it a 'wooden horse'—did not make much impression elsewhere: an ironical fact, since it turned out that with it Macmillan anticipated the rear-driven safety bicycle by almost forty years. It accumulated its myths—such as the one that Gorbals

Police Court fined Macmillan five shillings, following his trip to Glasgow and the injury of a child by riding on the pavement, and later refunded the fine to him as a tribute. It acquired, in a copy made about 1860 weighing 57lb, a rear-wheel brake, but during those twenty years from its origin little other work on the bicycle's general development was done.

In this period manumotives, manupedes (in which the drivers sat in *dos-à-dos* position) and treadle-driven quadricycles, ranging from a six-seat 'sociable' to a child's model—some of which were on exhibition at the Crystal Palace in London, 1851—did not advance principles of design. Nor did the one or two heavyweight tricycles. An old hobbyhorse, fitted with pedals and cranks to the front wheel by Karl Kech of Munich, unfortunately remained isolated, its importance in principle not recognised. The fact that another German, Philip Fischer, a teacher at Schweinfurt technical school, built a front-wheel-drive pedal cycle in or about 1852, with the accessories of brake, bell and luggage box, was not even generally known in Britain for over a hundred years. Copies had again been constructed locally and one of the few was sent for exhibition to the London Science Museum in 1958. Although experiment with the cycle, therefore, was not abandoned, pioneer efforts faded into oblivion.

The innovations of the decade which attracted attention were such events as the descent of a French 'mountebank' from a balloon at Tottenham—'a wanton risk of human life'—the insertion of a clause in the Cruelty to Animals Bill prohibiting the use of carts drawn by dogs—'unfair to costermongers'—a United States Congress law providing for conveyance of letters 'not more than three thousand miles by land' for three-halfpence; against a sporting background of Grand National Archery Fêtes at Shrewsbury before a large concourse of spectators, and the great matches between Gentlemen and Players of the Marylebone Cricket Club (*Illustrated London News*, 1854).

The idea of fitting cranks and pedals to the front wheel of an old wooden Draisienne being repaired, however, occurred to a Parisian perambulator and tricycle-maker, Pierre Michaux. Michaux suggested the crank 'like the crank handle of a grindstone', in 1861, and in that year his son, Ernest, built the prototype. So they converted the vélocifère of M Brunel, a Parisian hatter, into the first velocipede. The difference was that in this case the invention did not remain more or less in isolation. The bicycle now was launched as a practical machine. The following year 142 models were made, and within another three years annual production of the velocipede reached some four hundred machines, which sold at the equivalent of £8 each. Soon after, instead of the more rudimentary models, with wrought-iron backbone and iron tyres on equal-sized wheels, these machines were being made of damascened steel, fitted with ebony wheels, and ivory handle-grips. The saddle was mounted on a leaf spring, the cranks, slotted to allow variation of length, were fitted into counter-balanced pedals, and there was a lever shoe-brake on the rear tyre, operated by twisting a cord round the handlebar. A photograph of Ernest Michaux with a velocipede, c 1867, shows its enlarged driving wheel and lighter, but sturdy frame: its total weight was 59lb.

On the monument to Pierre and Ernest Michaux at the former's birthplace, Bar-le-Duc, near Verdun, a delightful cherub holds a model of the machine and they are commemorated as 'Inventeurs et propagateurs du vélocipède à pédale'.

Again the historical origin was obscured, this time by the claims of an employee, Pierre Lallement, who appeared on a modern 'bicycle', accompanied by an attendant on wheeled skates, in the Place de la Concorde and other parts of Paris. Whether he was working for Michaux in 1861 is in doubt, but in 1863, in apparent dissatisfaction at lack of recognition for ideas which he may well have contributed and which he said were appropriated, he left the firm and went to the USA. There, three years later, he was to take out a patent for the velocipede in association with James Carrol of New Haven, Connecticut, so achieving note as the first man to hold a bicycle patent in America (no 59915 USA). After his subsequent return to Paris and only moderate success in his own manufacturing business, Lallement again went to the USA and worked for the Pope Manufacturing Company, the founder in 1878 of the American cycle industry. His other claim, in relation to the velocipede, French historians discredit.

The firm of Michaux, père et fils, carried on their bicycle business until 1869 and exhibited machines at the Paris Exhibition of 1867. At the same exhibition the Paris agent of the Coventry Sewing Machine Company, Rowley Turner, was showing his firm's sewing machines. He brought back with him to Coventry, in November 1868, a Michaux velocipede and subsequently persuaded the sewing machine firm at Cheylesmore, of which his uncle was works manager, to manufacture four hundred machines of similar type for him to sell again in Paris, where production fell below demand. As Michaux had started the world's cycle industry (emulated by Lallement who provocatively called his business 'Ancienne Compagnie Vélocipèdienne'), so by the fortunes of war its centre was to be transferred from the Champs Elysées, Paris, to the Midlands of England. The outbreak of the Franco-Prussian War in 1870 killed French manufacture and closed this export market, forcibly diverting the sale of velocipedes to England. The Coventry Sewing Machine Company had by then been reconstructed in 1869 as the Coventry Machinists Company Ltd.

The Machinists did all they could to push the home trade, and the front-wheel-driven type rapidly became popular in spite of a price range of £10-£14. After the collapse of French industry Coventry, whose ribbon trade, employing at one time 18,000 looms, was then depressed and had begun to affect other kinds of business including watchmakers, increasingly welcomed this new form of enterprise. The machine, already attracting much attention in public, was now put under close scrutiny in the home of varied and under-deployed manufacturing skills. So French technical advances, and the skill of firms such as Michaux, Tribout and Meyer, Rousseau, Truffault as shown in the first cycle show at the Pré-Catalan, 1869, which included machines with wire spokes, spring-mounted front wheels, tubular frames and contracting-band brakes, received a critical setback, while English production got its impetus.

The 'Boneshaker', to give its English name, was at first of comparatively simple pattern (see plate, p35), but it had a more opportune start for commercial development than Macmillan's bicycle had enjoyed. Communications were better; the difference between Scotland's remoteness in 1840 and the links, by the railway and telegraph systems and by the technical press, both in this country and between Britain and France, of the 1860s was an important factor in disseminating knowledge of the Michaux machine, and of the products of the other Parisian or provincial cycle firms which had quickly sprung up. The *English Mechanic*, for example, a notable medium for inter-communication between inventors, first appeared on 31 March 1865; on 18 May 1866 it contained the first known and significant illustration of a tricycle driven by cranks and independent endless chain. The growth of light engineering with methods of large-scale production also made better techniques available for establishing a new industry. And at this point of Victorian progress, the time of the *nouveau riche*, more people were able to find the purchase price for a mode of transport which was practical rather than a *jouet d'enfant* or a rich man's toy like the hobbyhorse. The fact that it was regarded as a road vehicle at this stage is indicated by the fitting to one boneshaker offered to the public of a specially designed candle lamp for night travel. But road maintenance was another matter in a predominantly railway age.

The roads had been made to carry coach traffic and the tolls paid for their upkeep. When coaches stopped running, toll bars were closed and for a generation main roads fell into progressive decay. The traffic of farm waggon or squire's carriage, indifferent to or well-enough sprung to withstand the jolts, rolled in some of the 'repair' material but scattered the rest of the loose stones over the road. There might be cobbles at intervals or large sandstone setts such as can still be seen, on rare occasions, at bridges over or under canals. When tyres of solid rubber did become available they served rather to protect the rim of the boneshaker's wheel than the rider.

One of the Michaux machines was delivered in January 1869 to a gymnasium run by Charles Spencer in Old Street, London. When the frame and wheels had been assembled and the gymnasium cleared for action the spectators were astonished at the ease with which Mr Turner, grasping the handles and vaulting on to it with a short run, treadled his way round the room. Still greater was their astonishment when, after whirling round 'sitting on a bar above a pair of wheels that ought to fall down immediately he jumped off the ground', he slowly halted and, turning the front wheel diagonally, 'remained quite still balancing on the wheels'. Like many people at this time the spectators were sceptical of the possibility of remaining on two wheels 'arranged bicyclewise', and more so of holding the handle in any way except straight and in an unyielding manner. One of the spectators, however, John Mayall, a photographer of Regent Street, soon managed the machine well enough to ride on one, in company with Spencer and Turner (after a preliminary canter round Trafalgar Square) all the way from London to Brighton. Part of the journey down from Clayton to Brighton was covered at a speed of one mile in four minutes, despite a strong headwind. The feat was recorded in *The Times*, 19 February 1869, by a reporter who followed the riders as far as Crawley in a pair-horse carriage, and attracted a good deal of public attention. It showed the practicability of extended travel —the whole journey took about twelve hours—by their own leg power of amateurs in ordinary, untrained condition.

Charles Spencer subsequently produced a small manual, *The Bicycle: its use and action* (1870), in which he claimed to have introduced the bicycle into England, as well as to have been the first to 'master the seemingly difficult art of subjugating the two-wheeler'. Only the previous year a certain 'J.F.S.' had issued *How to Ride a Velocipede*—'Straddle a Saddle, then Paddle and Skedaddle'. And Rowley Turner, who when still a student in Paris in 1866 had become a proficient rider, was able to ride the machine he brought over from Coventry station to the Cheylesmore works.

In his manual a Charles Spencer velocipede 'of first-class manufacture only' was advertised as made of 'scrap iron, with hickory wheels, steel tires [sic] and balanced treadles, bearings fitted with double keys and screw nuts, pigskin saddle and carriage-painted, guaranteed for long journeys and hard wear'. It cost £12. Another model, recommended for ordinary use and racing, cost £10. Accessories and requisites were also offered—lamp, oilcan, shifting spanner, satchel and 'break cord'—as well as 'velocipede clothing'—flannel guernsey, drawers, serge trousers, half Wellington boots, short close-buttoned serge jacket. All were to be 'dark in colour on account of oiling the machine, and the boots must have thick soles with soft easy uppers, as walking in the hills cannot be avoided'. (The humorist's term 'velocipedestrian', for a rider was not without foundation.) This whole outfit and accessories could be had for £4 10s.

The fittest use of the bicycle [Spencer reminded his readers] is not to treat it as a toy, to be ridden on a smooth boarded surface, without impediment of any kind, and where all the riders are careful to follow each other in the same direction; but to use it as a vehicle, as an ordinary means of transit from one place to another, over roads rougher or smoother as the case may be. Thus, starting through the crowded streets at evening, as is my wont, and working at moderate speeds through omnibuses, cabs, drays, etc. etc. till gradually the road gets clearer, and extra steam may be put on [significant railway metaphor]: until at length the long country roads give full score for the greatest speed consistent with a due regard for the proposed length of journey, taking care, of course, not to be so exhausted at the end as to spoil all the pleasure.

This has been my practice for months on returning from business in the city to my residence at Harrow-on-the-Hill, and I can assure my readers that the 'Hill' occupies a very conspicuous part in the affair, particularly in wet or foggy weather, when it is a very different thing indeed to travel along dark, sloppy and hilly roads, to gliding swiftly round the brilliantly lighted and smooth area of the Agricultural Hall.

In some directions Spencer's enthusiasm perhaps ran away with him. His instructions included how to 'ride side-saddle, to ride without using legs or hands', and 'how to manage among London street traffic and in the country where horses shy at anything'. But for the ride to Brighton, performed on a 64lb boneshaker on the roads of that day, not all 'macadamised' even in theory, there can be nothing but admiration. He overdid his knowingness:

I have heard something of the 'instantaneous Break', but I can hardly fancy that the use of it can result in anything else than the introduction of an element of danger into the use of the bicycle: as it must be apparent to all that if you stop the Velocipede suddenly it must have much the same effect on it as on anything else in motion; and we all know that if a horse stops suddenly, as a matter of course the rider flies over its head, and this is the very result produced in Bicycle-riding: as in the races at the Agricultural Hall and elsewhere, riders have been seen to run against the railing at the end, and be instantly precipitated over amongst the audience. But of course we can hardly expect a mob of people to be always on hand to kindly break the fall with their persons. And when we are told that the invention has been rewarded with various prize medals, we can only wonder at the state of blissful ignorance with regard to the merits of a Bicycle in which the judges which awarded them must have been.

Spencer preferred to keep to the simple 'break', applied gradually, and was confident of stopping the back wheel even when going downhill, always provided that it was a properly proportioned machine and that the fittings were all secured by set nuts and linch-pins 'as in a locomotive'.

Other riders and makers of boneshakers were less strident in their claims and self-advertisement. No doubt a number of velocipedes were built by firms and enterprising blacksmiths in England before the Michaux came to Coventry. Thomas Smith & Sons, a large stamping firm in Birmingham, later claimed to be the founders of the bicycle and tricycle industry, as original makers of fittings and every part for the trade, established in 1848. Leaving aside how much of this claim applied to tricycles, there is no doubt that the first illustration of a two-wheeled machine appeared in the *English Mechanic* of 27 June 1867. There was also a Liverpool Velocipede Club apparently going strong in that same year, using American velocipedes. The earliest rubber tyres—flat or convex strips with canvas backing nailed on to the rim—were tested on snow-covered roads in England during November 1869. Boneshakers of a better quality than those copied from the French design were made by K. F. Hedges at Erith ironworks in 1869; a lady's version, which allowed her to use the side-saddle position and employed a double-throw crank on outrigger bearing, is to be seen in the Hove Museum. Among owner-riders of boneshakers were Prince Albert and Charles Dickens, the latter being taught to ride, it is claimed, by Charles Spencer.

Other forms also were tried, apart from the tricycles and quadricycles which continued to hold their own, or the later 'convertibles' —tricycles that could be made into four-wheelers (eg, by coupling the driving portions of a Cooper's Cruiser and a Humber tricycle). A counterweighted monocycle, 1869, is one example of efforts to produce a satisfactory single-wheel cycle, driven by cranks and pedals by a rider seated above the centre of a large wheel. One

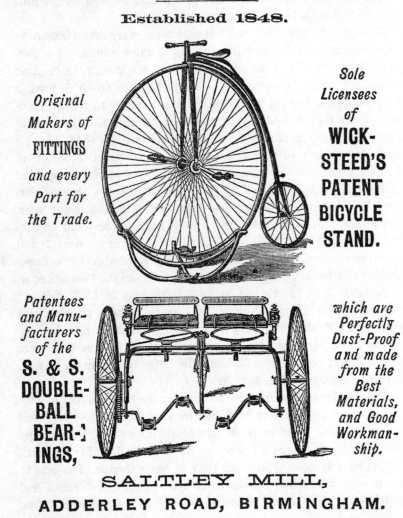
Advertisement in Charles Spencer's The Bicycle Road Book (1881)

such rider in curly-brimmed bowler, tartan jacket and strap trousers appears in a contemporary print, pedalling along the road-way in front of villa residences his solid twelve-spoke wheel with its iron blocks on fork extensions. A patent for a monocycle, in which the rider sat *inside* the 8ft wheel on the axle, was taken out in the USA, also in 1869. The usual place for the monocycle was the circus ring, where patrons of Astley's enjoyed its more spec-tacular use. (Later it was the penny-farthing that provided the trick mount for such riders as Ermina Chelli of the Cirque d'Eté, *c* 1887.) The dicycle, which had two equal wheels mounted parallel on a common spindle, appeared in prototype in 1866, a model with ten-foot diameter wheels, two T-shaped handles and a loop in the axle to support the rider, who had originally to propel this machine by using his feet against the ground as with the hobby-horse. It was to make a stronger practical bid for acceptance to-wards the end of the next decade, when a saddle, above and behind the axle, pedal cranks, pulleys and steel belts to the two driving wheels were incorporated in a machine patented by E. F. C. Otto, of which about a thousand were manufactured.

Before this progressive decade closed, the first bicycle race on record in England had been run near the Welsh Harp, at Hendon, on Whit Monday 1868, and the prize of a silver cup won by Arthur Markham. The first official bicycle race, held at St Cloud, Paris, one day before that, was won by an Englishman, James Moore, over the distance of 1,200 metres. The same rider, then living in Paris, succeeded also out of a field of two hundred starters (including five women) in winning the world's first long-distance road race from Paris to Rouen, 83 miles, in November the follow-ing year. His time was 10hr 25min. One of the first exhibitions and race meetings of velocipedes was held in Studley Royal Park, near Fountains Abbey, Yorkshire, in June 1869: a prize of £4 was offered for the best bicycle, £2 for the best three-wheeler; points of superiority included leg-guard, self-acting lubricator and pedometer.

The year 1869 saw also the beginnings of Le Véloce Club de Paris, publication of the first cycling periodical, *Le Vélocipède Illustré*, and the opening of the race track at Crystal Palace. Rowley Turner won the first race there on the gravel track and also won the first race at the Agricultural Hall, Islington, on boards. He had won a medal in the Paris-Rouen race and had also the more unusual distinction of making first use of a bicycle in actual warfare. It provided his means of retreat from Paris, under Prussian fire, after departure of the last train during the fateful—so far as the British cycle industry was concerned—Franco-German war. The bicycle already had a foot, or rather a spoke, in the social and military life of the times.

The pundits saw in bicycling advantages for all classes: for country clergymen and doctors, road surveyors and 'letter-carriers'; for all who had long rounds to perform and with this aid to locomotion could do their ten or twenty miles with 'scarcely any fatigue'. There was no doubt about the healthiness of the exercise, and as to the difficulties of learning, they were not greater than those of horse-riding, skating or swimming, while the acquisition of bicycling ability placed a man of ordinary strength in a position superior to that of the professional jockey. No exercise was so good for the development of the muscles of the arms, legs and back—indeed, if bicycling continued to increase in popularity, even Mr Disraeli might have to withdraw his lament that 'the British race is in a state of physical decline.'

In its wider effects bicycling was to be in no small way revolutionary. Before the advent of the bicycle of the 1860s the great majority of people had been limited to familiarity with and enjoyment of their immediate geographical and social circumstances. When cycle development led to a steady supply of discarded models, the cheap second-hand machine became a feasible means of transport—instead of slow carrier's cart, costly horse or relatively high train fare—and the desire to travel away from industrial centres was augmented by this new possibility. Other former barriers were also shown to be no longer insurmountable, such as the convention of rigid Sabbath observances, stiff and stuffy proprieties in exchange between the sexes, confining and cumbrous modes of dress, class distinctions of the 'keep-us-in-our-proper-stations' order. Means available to freedom in one direction helped to develop the urge to freedom in others.

The last year of the decade was a notable one for the velocipede in America, at any rate as far as print and popular song went. The *Velocipedist* was started in New York and at least a dozen songs are on record, some with lyrics, some without, celebrating the riders and their machines. The 'Velocipedia Waltz', various velocipede galops, 'The Flying Velocipede', 'The Unlucky Velocipedist', 'Velocipediana' are a few of them.

> Whoop la, out of the way
> We come with lightning speed,
> There's nothing like the rattling gait
> Of the flying velocipede.

One of the cover pictures to a Galop shows two dandies leading a group of well-dressed men in top hats on boneshakers; another shows a woman rider wearing bloomers, for which the craze, started in America in 1850, really came into its own in the 1890s. 'The Unlucky Velocipedist' simply shows a rider on a wooden-spoked machine and has no words. Perhaps the chorus of the Velocipede song, from a burlesque 'Sinbad the Sailor', hits the mode off best:

> It never runs away
> And it doesn't take much to feed;
> It's thoroughly reliable—
> The new velocipede;
> Upon the way you work your legs
> And feet depends its speed;
> And that's about the total of
> The new Velocipede.

In 1869 the 'Great-Wheel-Hoss-I-Pede' or the 'New Sensation' was sung by W. F. Collins of the original Christy Minstrels at St James' Hall. The song's coloured cover, by the celebrated Alfred Concanen, shows six minstrels all riding boneshakers, and is now a coveted collector's piece.

Perhaps the last word should be taken from a contemporary colour print in the writer's possession, of a boneshaker rider in cutaway coat, hard hat, yellow waistcoat and purple trousers, whose cut-out paper legs can be set in motion by a simple trigger device. He is shown among the dundreary-whiskered drivers of 'patent safety hansom cabs', above the verse:

> As a man fond of pleasure and ease,
> Why ride then on Velocipedes?
> Better stop at home and comfort your Wife
> Who *ought* to be the joy of your life.

Page 35 : (above) Boneshaker; (below) Ordinary

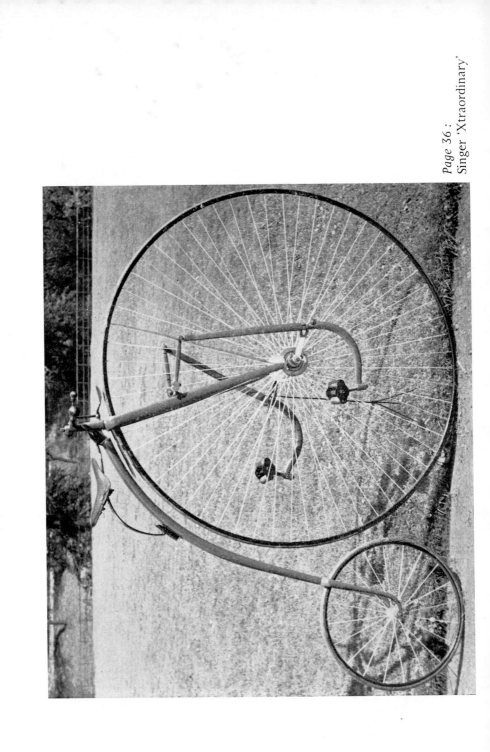

CHAPTER THREE

ORDINARIES

THE IMPETUS to English production of boneshakers, or
'timber trucks' and 'treadmills' as they were derogatively called,
and to the industry's early location in Coventry had been provided
by chance and Rowley Turner. The improvements and modifications
to these strong but weighty and crude machines were provided by
the fertile brains and mechanical expertise of a number of men and
firms in Coventry and London. Draisiennes, and at first velocipedes,
had wheels of equal size, although the later improved boneshaker
might have a rear wheel of 30in in diameter and front wheel of 36in
(as well as a seat more nearly over the pedals to improve thrust,
and wider handlebars for better steering control): according to the
evidence of an advertisement by Charles Spencer the front wheel
could be as much as 48in. (Magee of Paris produced in 1869 a
48in-24in wheeled machine made entirely of iron, steel and rubber.)

The aim of improvers was, in general, to reduce weight, ease
propulsion and make it possible to achieve higher speeds by increasing the diameter of the driving wheel. Several intermediate
developments contributed to one or other of these aims, before the
logical conclusion was reached of a radically different form of

C

machine. An important innovation was that taken out under patent in 1869 for 'wheels constructed on the suspension principle'. The 'Phantom' bicycle, invented by W. F. Reynolds and J. H. Mays of Tower Hill, London, had, instead of all-wood wheels, wire spokes in pairs threaded through an 'eye' screwed into the wooden rims and held between two halves of the hub flange. Instead of the old heavy backbone the frame was a triangulated one, built up from iron rods, and hinged between the two wheels, which moved independently—a novel if somewhat tricky means of steering which enabled the machine to be turned in a small circle. Thick rubber tyres, cemented on, and sprung front forks added to road comfort, and there were footrests for use in running downhill. The total weight was 53lb. Although the suspended wheel was not an entirely new idea—early nineteenth-century waterwheels were often built in the same way—it was new in application to the bicycle. When it was found that wooden wheel rims did not remain true, iron rims were substituted. In silhouette the 'Phantom' has the elegant lines of the well-sprung curricle, now in greater refinement.

The wheels of the 'Ariel' made by Haynes & Jefferies, Coventry, to a design patented by James Starley of the Coventry Machinist Company and William Hillman, and introduced in September 1871, had a device for tensioning the spokes. Starley's 'ribbon' spokes made from sheet brass were used at first, then strips of steel, and then roundwire. Although individual spokes in the suspension wheel could not be tightened, a cross-bar brazed to the spindle between the hub flanges with adjustable tie-rods, joining its ends to the wheel's rim, made it possible to tighten all spokes at once. The 'Ariel' sold at a price of £8 and the first round rubber tyres were made for it, spongy on the underside, tougher on the tread, by J. L. Hancock. With a 'speed gear', which permitted two revolutions of the front wheel for one of the pedal cranks, the cost was £12. Although some of the machines on show at the Paris Exhibition in 1867 reputedly had speed gears, this first British patent speed gear was another Starley invention: he had also evolved the 'Ariel's' centre steering-head to supersede the old boneshaker socket type, which tended to swing round and trap the rider's leg.

On a bicycle of this type James Moore, the Paris-Rouen race winner, covered 14 miles 440yd in one hour, the best performance up to date (1873). A front wheel of 48in and a rear wheel of 22in gave the machine an appearance heralding that of the Ordinary: the weight was 51½lb.

From the number of his inventions and modifications leading to its improvement James Starley (1830-81) well earned the title 'Father of the Cycle Industry' and, after his death, an impressive monument in his adopted city of Coventry. The long scroll spring, extending in front of the steering head, a feature of the Coventry Machinists Company's leading model the 'Gentleman's Bicycle', was his; as was the mounting step, used as long as the Ordinary itself, the rubber-covered wooden pedals instead of heavy cast brass, made triangular in form so as to present always a pedal face to the foot, and the footrests on stays in front of the enlarged driving wheel. The apparition in out of the way places up and down England of what, according to *Punch's* countryman, looked like 'a man a-ridin' upon nawthin' ', was in no small way due to Starley's gift for mechanics.

In the same year as that of the 'Ariel's' appearance an improvement of the means of spoke tightening was introduced in a machine called the 'Tension' bicycle, designed by W. H. J. Grout of Stoke Newington. By nipple adjustment at the rim the spokes on this machine could be tightened individually instead of all simultaneously, a method afterwards that was generally accepted. The 'Tension' also included, among its other improvements, hollow front forks, hollow rubber tyres vulcanised to the rim, a pedal for use with the ball of the foot, and cranks connected directly to the hub. Front wheel dimensions of 48in to rear wheel of 24½in were typical, but models were available with the driving wheel up to 60in in diameter. The 'Tension' weighed 69lb.

Coventry 'Spiders', as Starley's 1872 models with radial spokes were called, and 'Tensions' were serviceable mounts. The dependability of the 'Tension' was demonstrated when, on 2 June 1873, four 'tourists' set out to ride on four of them from London to John O' Groats House, the most northerly point of the British Isles. In weather which was good, bad, very bad or merely wet and windy, and on variable roads, they accomplished the feat on 16 June, covering on some days as much as sixty or seventy miles, on others little more than twenty, in the first really long-distance road ride on record. They were financed by a London cycle manufacturer, James Sparrow, who organised their 800 mile ride. Such feats not only underlined the value of the machines, but stimulated demand for production from a now rapidly developing trade. New ideas for improvement were thrown up—Starley's tangent spoke wheel, now normal, was one; ball bearings instead of plain or cone bearings for the wheel spindle another. These were applied to front-wheel spindles in the first place and improved on later by James Moore. As a contemporary saw it, 'a bicycle, since the arrangement of springs, brakes and rubber tyres have removed half the terrors of ruts and steep gradients, is more useful than the cleverest nag man ever bestrode, with the additional advantage that a bicycle consumes nothing but a little oil.'

The high bicycle (or 'Ordinary' as it was termed later in the 1870s) was not specifically invented, but evolved. By about the middle of that decade the names of English bicycle-making firms included Coventry Machinists Co, later to be known as the Swift Cycle Company—by far the largest firm—Thomas Humber of Nottingham, Hydes & Wigfull, Sheffield, makers of the high-class polished steel 'Stanley' bicycle and inventors of the 'Stanley head' in most general use, Ellis & Company of Farringdon Street, John Keen of Surbiton, known for the height and lightness of his machines, Dan Rudge of Wolverhampton (amalgamating in 1880 with the Tangent and Coventry Tricycle Company, formerly Haynes & Jefferies), George Singer of Coventry, who had been a foreman in the Coventry Sewing Machine Company's works and was an early associate of Starley, and Smith & Starley, in business at the St John's Works, Coventry. About twenty firms in all were following the business. By the end of the decade the well-made, full-size high bicycle was a sophisticated machine with hollow tube sections, brazed U-section rims, ball or roller bearings, reduced trailing wheel and direct front-wheel drive, providing a high gear ratio between pedals and wheel, from a 60in or even larger front wheel according to the rider's length of leg. It was reasonably light, strong and simple, the engine being the rider, and what 'works' there were serving merely to transmit his energy, with little mechanical loss or noise.

A typical later Ordinary was the Howe Spider, built by the Howe Machine Company, Glasgow, and on view in the Museum of Transport there. A sample advertisement of this period reads:

Bicycles: New and Secondhand. Manufacturers of the Nonsuch and Nancy Lee, the best and cheapest machines as yet manufactured. The No 3 Nonsuch, fitted with all improvements, price £6.5s, less 15 per cent for cash or supplied on easy terms. Price lists free. Agent for the Humber, Premier, Woodcock, Tangent and all the best makers. Over two hundred machines, Bicycles and Tricycles, both new and secondhand on view in our showrooms. [South London Machinists Company.]

Until the mid-1870s it was bicycles not tricycles that predominated in both popularity, technical development and supply.

The high-wheeled bicycle was introduced to America by English firms exhibiting at the Continental Exposition at Philadelphia, 1876. Colonel Albert A. Pope of Boston visited London and Coventry to study bicycle construction. He returned with samples of English wheels and then bought a sewing-machine factory at Hartford to convert into a bicycle factory in 1878. The

Boston firm of Cunningham, Heath & Company also imported and sold English makes of bicycles in the USA. Pope's subsequently well-known 'Columbia' had a rival in the 'Victor', produced by the Overman Wheel Company also of Boston, Massachusetts, 1886.

ON ROAD AND TRACK

Riding the Ordinary—price range from £6 as quoted to £20—was not for everyone. Although in Coventry, the peculiar home of cycling, 'it is fast becoming the custom for workmen to go home on their bicycles during the dinner hour', to many if it was not too expensive it was too risky, and, for the unathletic, too difficult. Clubs, of course, and racing flourished. The Pickwick Cycling Club, London, one of the earliest and longest surviving, was founded in the boneshaker days of 1870. The Bicycling Touring Club, begun in Harrogate in the second year of the annual meet there, August 1878, became five years later the Cyclists' Touring Club or CTC. From 1881 one of the most popular social events was a 'camp meet' at Harrogate, and before the decade was out the CTC could claim to be the largest athletic association in the world, with over 20,000 members. Whilst the CTC obviously provided answers to the tourist's problems, the Bicycle Union, formed in 1878, and soon merged in the NCU (National Cycling Union) dealt with legal, political and organisational matters which affected cycling and the cyclist. In the same year the First British Cycle Show, the Stanley Bicycle Show, was held at Camden Town and provided Victorian enthusiasts with all the excitement that the Motor Show offers us today.

By 1880 there were some 230 clubs established in all parts of Britain: Cambridge University Club alone had 280 members. A photograph dated September 1879 shows an American bicycle club on the road at Readville, Massachusetts, one of the dozen or so then existent in the USA. Boston BC was the first founded and helped to make Boston the early centre of bicycling. The League of American Wheelmen was formed in 1880. To detail the origins and activities of the local clubs is beyond the scope of this book, but a few of the notable and early ones may be mentioned. Active in the early seventies were the 'Amateur', the 'Tension', the Middlesex, the Surrey, the Brighton, the 'True Briton' (Northampton), the 'Dark Blue' (Oxford), the 'Sun' (Wolverhampton), the Newcastle-on-Tyne velocipede club, and, claiming to be the oldest club in existence, the 'Aston Star' (Birmingham). A published record of the Anfield Bicycle Club, Liverpool, provides much lively detail of personalities, performances and manifestations of club spirit.

The fact that the roads, apart from such main ones as those from London to Bath, to Dover and to the north were, to say the least, uneven in standard and at times came little short of calamitous, tried, tested, but did not deter the Ordinary clubman. McAdam's prescription that no stone ought ever to be cast upon a road for the purpose of repairing it which could not be put in a man's mouth—small stones under pressure of traffic fit each other's angles and soon pack into a hard mass—was probably as often recognised in the breach as in the observance, on minor roads. Notes on the road in a *Text Book for Riders* (1874) makes frequent reference to perilous conditions all over the country:

Liverpool to Prescot, 8 miles good road, then within 6 miles of Newcastle-under-Lyne a very bad bit full of holes . . . after leaving Lichfield there is a very trying road, short lengths being good and bad alternately. . . . From Mansfield to Doncaster stiff clay, very rutty and uneven. Tadcaster to York it is quite impassable. From York to Knaresborough it is in some places three inches deep in mud, but improves to Ripley, there to Ripon is perfect . . .

From Peterboro' to Market Deeping the road was very bad, but gradually improved to Spalding: from Rivesby to Horncastle nearly all loose flint: after this the road degenerates into two wheel ruts and a horse track, driving [ie riding] being sometimes impossible . . .

43

The weather being wet found the roads after Herne Hill very pasty, very indifferent to Bromley and worse to Farnboro'.

Sometimes despair almost creeps in :

The road between Birmingham and Wolverhampton is very bad and wearying : in fact it is full of holes and tramway ruts. The bicyclist had better train this bit . . .
Shrewsbury to Nantwich is simply execrable and for 45 miles further.

On the other hand, occasionally a cheerful note breaks in to show what could be achieved. Half way between Thrapstone and Huntingdon it is at first rather loose on the surface, but soon alters into a well-made gravel road. Huntingdon to Cambridge is considered the finest road in England for bicyclists, being very level and smooth.

In those days, before county council maintenance teams with steam rollers, it was the habit to dump the broken stones across the road and leave them to be worn in by the traffic, the time usually chosen for dumping being early summer so that the tourist traffic should do its fair share of the rolling. Loose stones, often of considerably more than regulation size, were the chief sources of cyclists' mishaps—apart from loose tyres, thorns jammed in the forks, dogs and straying hens. Holes roughly filled in with varied materials—granite, earth, chalk, flints, quagmires of mud, hard-packed middles with loose, stony edges—were indeed such constant hazards that in the mid-eighties an area meeting of the NC was called at Birmingham, to try either to devise a remedy or to agitate for radical action. After test cases, with certain road surveyors brought before magistrates for failing to keep their roads in order, had strengthened their hand, the NCU and CTC formed a 'Roads Improvement Association': both horse users and horse owners as well as cyclists gave the movement strong backing. Its declared objects were: to circulate popular and technical road literature in order to enlighten ratepayers on a subject vitally affecting their pockets and interests; and to guide county councillors, highway boards and their employees about proper road repair and maintenance; to remonstrate with responsible authorities where neglect of roads became a public scandal and take legal action where necessary; to watch or introduce fresh legislation to remove anomalies; and to take up the question of fingerposts and milestones and their erection and maintenance.

From 1880 the Bicycle Union also began to erect 'Danger' boards at the top of dangerously steep or rutted hills, a task continued by the NCU and CTC jointly from 1887-97 and thereafter by the CTC alone. By 1903 when the Motor Car Act provided for the erection of road signs by county councils the CTC had put up 2,331 Danger and 1,989 Caution signs, with white lettering on either a red or a blue background.

One of the major stumbling blocks in the cycling organisations' crusade to obtain better road surfaces lay in the distinction, in highway law, between 'non-feasance' and 'mis-feasance'. If the work done by an authority on the highway was done negligently and someone was shown to have suffered injury in consequence, that was 'mis-feasance' and the said authority was liable to damages. If, however, as was to become the case, an authority was legally bound to repair its roads but neglected to do so and someone suffered injury in consequence, that was 'non-feasance' and the injured party was not able to claim damages.

The doctrine of 'non-feasance' had its historical origin in the days before highway authorities or their predecessors, highway surveyors, when the maintenance of highways was the responsibility of the inhabitants of a county, ie 'the inhabitants at large'. No action, it was held in a case brought against Men of Devon (1788), could be maintained against a fluctuating body of persons. In 1892 the House of Lords confirmed, in an action brought against Newmarket Local Board, that even the transfer to a highway authority of the obligation to repair did not render it liable to action for results of 'non-feasance'.

There is no distinction in Scotland between non-feasance and mis-feasance: in 1939 the Alness Committee on Road Accidents recommended that the law of England in this respect be brought into line therefore with Scottish law. When a new Highway Act reached the statute book twenty years later the General Council of the Bar strongly recommended again this same thing. Defective highways were still causing minor injuries, cut tyres, dented rims etc which the statisticians probably never heard about and for which the cyclist had no redress under the doctrine of non-feasance=non-liability.

Of the perils which attended on the bicycle pioneer of the seventies before legal rights were defined, the attention of boys with a stone thrown, a cap flicked or a stick thrust between the spokes were the least obnoxious. Tramps were ever ready to take advantage of a mishap on a lonely road, roughs—known then as 'road hogs'—were wont to molest a single cyclist in the streets, and magistrates, in some of the urban areas, became notorious for their 'anti-cyclist' attitudes. Patrols of mounted police made raids on bicyclists frequenting the wood-paved roads of Hammersmith and Kensington: fines for 'furious riding' were imposed, usually to the maximum of 40 shillings. One case involving the St Albans coach was not untypical of the times. The guard of this vehicle actually provided himself with a slung shot at the end of a strong rope, fastened to the coach, which he could fling into the wheels of any passing bicycle. *He* was, at length, brought to book.

Nevertheless, club runs and record-breaking road rides were among the highlights of all-male sporting life of this period. For outings and meets there were set rules and observances. The club captain took his place at the head of the formation, members took position behind according to seniority, the sub-captain bringing up the rear. Both these prestige positions might be determined by racing results. All members wore the uniform of the club, usually a jacket and ribbon or badge and diminutive cap (see plate, p72). Anfielders, for instance, wore black with a little 'hussar' braiding on the jacket, and stripes of royal blue on a black scarf; the various officers had silver monograms, that of the captain being gold. Catford 'Kitters' sported claret and gold. The captain had entire control, with a bugler to convey orders to members, and for the public safety might compel members to stop or dismount when passing horses etc. Some clubs fined members who infringed this rule and suspended them until the fine had been paid. 'When four members or more are mounted they should ride two abreast and such a distance shall be kept as shall allow the right-hand man to fall to the rear of his left-hand man in case of single file being necessary and in all cases to obey the rules of the road'.

These rules were at first a constant source of trouble, since a local authority could impose its own bylaws for cycling. Some required a bell, others a whistle warning; lamps in some places must be lit at sunset, earlier in others or, it might be, an hour later. Only after long labour did the NCU succeed in obtaining universal bylaws for regulation of cycle traffic. A paragraph from a provincial newspaper, 1877, from a man who had been knocked down by a bicycle whilst out walking with his wife through a Northamptonshire village on a Sunday afternoon, made a plea not only for magistrates' restriction and control, but for a five-shilling tax so as to impose registration of riders and some protection to pedestrians.

The outings, as apart from matches, even in early Coventry Spider days might be considerable expeditions. Some members of the Amateur Bicycle Club, for example, had an autumn outing in 1871 from Putney to Oxford, Gloucester, the Wye Valley, Abergavenny, Carmarthen, Aberayron, Aberystwith, Dolgelly, Festiniog, Bangor, Conway and Chester. They took twelve days over it, returning to London in five via Llanrwst, Shrewsbury, Worcester and Oxford. No great day's performance was done, but a long distance was traversed and the party had time to visit objects of interest and enjoy the lovely scenery—despite the vicissitudes of Welsh hills and a species of road 'in places no better than a neglected watercourse'. The following year another club member, calling himself 'Dauntless', rode from Liverpool to London, 206 miles in two days, on a 48in Spider. A cycling publication of 1874, offering advice on continental tours, included not only Belgium, Holland, France and the Rhineland, but also the western and northern cantons of Switzerland, even though 'the bicycle does not love mountains and mountains are, in two senses, the most prominent features of Switzerland.'

There were such 'golden rules for bicycle riders' on tour as 'Never travel a long journey without having your drawers lined smoothly and carefully with chamois leather or buckskin'. 'Never ride in the early morning fasting: a little rum and milk with an egg beaten up in it is an excellent sustenant.' 'Never place your foot on the rest for a ride down hill which you cannot see all the way to the bottom, without having your machine thoroughly in hand.' 'Never ride in the dark unless compelled to do so.' 'Never fail, when resting on a journey, to place your machine beyond the reach of meddlesome hands.'

The 'classic' highway for a short run was the old Portsmouth road, the section as far as Ripley being a regular promenade on a Sunday morning. One of the main reasons for its popularity was the 'Anchor Inn' at Ripley, discovered by Jack Keen, a bicycle maker and rider par excellence, and thereafter made a rendezvous by racing and cycling clubs. About the turn of the century some hundred 'wheelmen' would lunch there on Sundays and the Ripley run or rally is a tradition still kept up by the Southern Veteran-Cycle Club on old-time machines.

Inter-club matches and races, held at first under the auspices of the Amateur Athletic Club until the formation of the Bicycle Union, whetted and amply exercised members' keenness. An amateur bicycle race over a course of four miles was held annually at the Lillie Bridge track, London. Between 1871, the year of the first championship race, and 1875, H. P. Whiting was the winner on four occasions, riding a Keen machine. (Jack (John) Keen, professional champion: 50 miles in 3hr 5min 45sec in 1876.) On the other occasion Whiting did not compete and after 1875 he relinquished amateur status. His time for this race improved from 16min 25sec to 14min 37sec. Another star of the Lillie Bridge ground, the professional David Stanton, gave in 1874 what the press hailed as 'the most extraordinary performance on record of any man, animal or machine—106 miles in 7hr 58min 54½sec.'

From 1878 onwards British amateur championships inaugurated by the Bicycle Union were held, and after a year replaced the AAC race. They were run off over different distances at various tracks in London and the provinces. Of the races held in the first three years H. L. Cortis of the Wanderers Club was the outstanding winner, taking altogether seven first places over distances of 1, 5, 25 and 50 miles on an 'Invincible'. In 1881 G. Lacy Hillier, an outstanding personality in the cycling world and editor of *Bicycle News*, brought honour to the Stanley Club by sweeping the board over all four distances on a Humber. The next year Cortis became the first man to ride 20 miles in one hour on a bicycle. Of the eighty races at various distances between 1878 and 1890 over fifty were won on Humber bicycles, which still employed radial spoking.

Apart from these national events challenges between Cambridge and Oxford club members led to an inter-university race, the course being the 84 miles between those seats of sporting enthusiasm. Clubs, of course, and individuals were constantly putting out challenges and achieving new performances, so that there grew up a wide variety of trophy events. Such team matches as that held between the Surrey and Middlesex bicycle clubs, with six riders apiece striving to obtain the united best result between London and Brighton and back, led to remarkable times for the Ordinary of that day (1873). The first man home, from Middlesex, covered the 134 miles in 11 hours on a 52in wheel machine, but the other team won by filling second and third places. When, in August 1874, the Middlesex club held a race for its captaincy and sub-captaincy, the course was the 105 miles from Bath to London, and the start, made with some difficulty owing to the great number of people assembled, was at 5 am from in front of Bath Abbey. Although some competitors had to dismount and walk up Box Hill, all passed through Chippenham at 14 mph and made no stop till Marlborough (32m). The two leading riders covered the first 50 miles in 4¾ hours, but arrivals at the club house, Kensington, left no doubt about the captain-to-be. He came over two and a half hours in advance of the next man, his future 'sub'.

In 1880 Surrey Bicycle Club inaugurated a hill-climbing competition, a type of event which took the fancy of many other clubs. The Surrey climb was up Reigate Hill, a total distance of 2,640yd, total rise of 420ft and average gradient of 4½/100 with the steepest stretch 12/100. H. L. Cortis rode it with one arm in a sling and the winner, G. H. Coleman, ran out in 4min 40sec. Muswell Hill was another favourite venue as was Wizard Hill at Alderley Edge.

The flavour of cycling in the late seventies and early eighties, the period of the tennis parties, picnics, sport and club life of the upper- and upper-middle-class English society portrayed by George du Maurier in *Punch*, comes out well in the reminiscences of A. W. Rumney. Sometime honorary secretary of the Cambridge University Bicycle Club, Rumney learned to ride in 1876 on a borrowed 46in wheel 'Challenge', and was lucky enough to buy, for only £3, a 48in Devey, 'the working man's bicycle', to ride about his home, Keswick in Cumberland, between the pursuits of tennis, swimming, football, walking and climbing. Then he bought himself Sturmey's *Indispensable Handbook for Cyclists* (1879) and when sent to school in Surrey 'went heart and soul into cycling'. By then he had abandoned the Devey for a 50in Club with roller bearings to the front wheel, cones to the back, a rubber insulated spring and a front-wheel roller brake actuated by twisting the handlebar.

Beside scouring the whole country I practised diligently at tracks and slow riding and became really master of that very excellent mount. I also attended the Hampton Court meet, along with some 2,000 other riders, riding with a little band of BTC-ites who had no other club. I was considered too young to join the Sutton BC which contained such good riders as C. Crute and Sydney Lee. The most enthusiastic rider of the suburb was, however, the barber, who rode regularly every morning before breakfast and was reputed to have once spoken to the great Cortis. It was in this year that Lacy Hillier won all the championships, but I had not yet become a racing 'fan' and never rode over to the Surbiton track to see those held there. In this year was held the first Cyclists' Camp at Harrogate, the forerunner of a long series of those highly popular junkettings, which for some incomprehensible reason have gone completely out of fashion.

In the summer holidays I won my first race, a slow one, the result of my constant practising on the Cheam road, Sutton. . . . I think it was the same summer Cockermouth was celebrating its adoption of electric lighting—I fancy the first town to do so and it was a failure even on the first night— by holding a race meeting and procession, that I was appointed Consul for Keswick by J. T. Smith of Kendal and entitled to wear a surround of red velvet to my shield badge. I also blossomed into a real cycling suit of the blue serge almost universally worn in those days. When I returned to Sutton in the autumn I was fortunate in finding another boarder and him I quickly initiated into the art. He was somewhat short-sighted and his parents would only allow him to cycle on a Safety [sic] and as the only one available in those days was the Xtra Challenge, he went up to town and got a 50in of that make for about £10. The cranks were worked by levers attached to the highly raked forks, and now and again these levers would double-joint backwards in a disconcerting way. Another trouble common to all solid-tyred cycles was the frequent loosening of the tyre from the rim. The remedy was Prout's Elastic Glue applied with the aid of a red-hot poker.

In the spring of '82 we blossomed out in BTC uniform—green serge suits, Norfolk jackets, knee breeches, stockings and stiff helmets, £2 1s complete. Resplendent in them we attended the Hampton Court meeting in May, riding with a score or two of other BTC-ites between the real club men and the unattached. Of course the Xtra chose the time of the procession to turn one of its levers inside out and we had to fall out. Occasionally we spent Saturday afternoons at race meetings at the Crystal Palace, seeing my subsequent friends, J. S. Whatton and Keith Falconer, win the Five Miles and Fifty Miles championships respectively. On another occasion when Cortis beat the mile record in 2min 43sec at the Palace, I had a shot at the slow race under very different conditions to those at Cockermouth.

Some of the machines especially designed for racing appear formidable mounts. The 'Invincible' with its 54in driving wheel and diminutive trailing wheel, the 56in Humber racer (1889), the 59in Rudge, 'a comparatively whippy bicycle', and even the larger Humber Roadster with a 62in wheel (c 1885), built probably for a CU Clubman, the Hon Ion Keith Falconer who became NCU two-mile champion, and suitable for someone at least 6ft 6in in height : these were 'High Wheelers', as the Americans termed them, for athletes, and impressive machines on the track. The vaulting method being too difficult, in competitions a 'starting stool' was used to mount them, later giving place to an assistant 'pusher off'. Weights varied from 50lb for the last mentioned Humber down to 26lb for the Beeston Humber racer and only 22lb for the 'Invincible'—one of the lightest Ordinaries ever built. (Up to 1880 a 35lb machine was generally considered to be as light as it was possible to make consistent with strength and stability, but racing men's insistence on further reduction obtained it—at the expense of breakdown or injury to heavy men mounted on flimsy racers.)

Cortis was mounted on such a lightweight 'Invincible' for his hour record; it was built by the Surrey Machinists Company. So far as front-wheel size goes, however, James Starley's famous 'Ariel'

Page 53 : (*above*) Crypto 'Bantam'; (*below*) Columbia shaft drive

Page 54 : G. P. Mills, on the Humber tricycle on which he beat the Land's End to John O'Groats record

special with a 7ft wheel, driven by rods hinged to the fork with pedals some inches above wheel centre, and ridden by him to a Whit Monday meet at Leamington, was manifestly in a class by itself.

By 1885 there were about two hundred firms making Ordinaries and, according to contemporary estimates, based on CTC reports —a body which now had its chief officer in every large town and minor official in most sizeable villages—about 400,000 cyclists in Britain. The writer's grandfather was one of them. He recalled losing control of a 'penny farthing', the Cockney nickname which stuck to Ordinaries from the nineties onwards, and careering down a steep hill to a side road at right angles near the bottom. As the brake was no use he attempted the turn, hit an eight-foot wall, somersaulted over and was 'out' with concussion for the next two days. Such accidents—'headers', 'nose-overs', 'croppers' or 'imperial crowners'—were far from uncommon even on more level ground. 'Falling forwards from a bicycle is by no means a difficult exploit', wrote Viscount Bury in his introduction to the 'Cycling' volume of the *Badminton Library of Sports and Pastimes* (1887); 'indeed the difficulty is to avoid performing it.' Not only was getting off in orthodox fashion difficult, but getting on and steering presented problems for learners also. Consequently, several manuals of instruction came out and there were agencies or 'academies' where riding was taught in most big towns.

A beginning was usually made on a boneshaker, an assistant with a stout rope attached to the handle running beside the novice and pulling on it in emergency, to obviate an injurious fall with the solid iron-framed machine crashing on to the rider's legs. Anxious to obtain more speed with the same amount of labour the tyro, of course, would go on to the Ordinary as soon as possible, mounting with support from a rail or post—not using the step at first— dismounting with the assistant's guidance of his left foot to the step, and being careful to avoid putting his toe among the spokes.

D

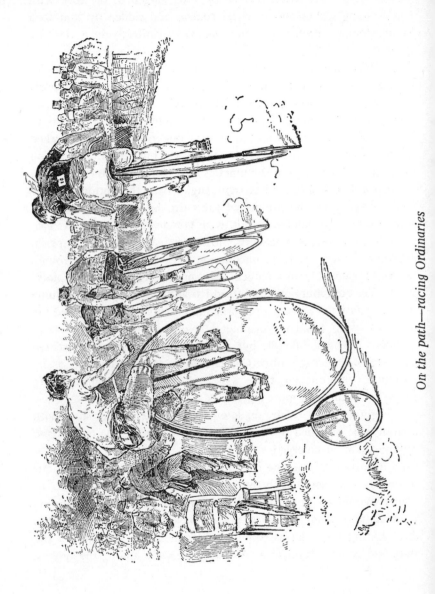

On the path—racing Ordinaries

Pedalling at first by jerky effort tended to thrust the wheel out of course, putting a severe strain on the hands and arms; and when in danger of a fall it was fatally easy to turn away from the threatened danger instead of slightly turning the front wheel *into* its direction. Heavily built men were cautioned against trying to mount by a spring off the step, as it might severely damage the machine ridden, 'the backbone of which will often become twisted unless it has been made especially strong'. Later on perhaps, a rider could try throwing the right leg over the handlebar instead of over the backbone to dismount, so as not to be hampered by a rising pedal.

Style and 'science' in riding the Ordinary were acquired only with considerable practice. The upright posture, the merits of bent arms versus the 'straight pull' on the handles, the 'over-grip', the 'under-grip' (for speed), the art of ankling, of steering with the feet only, of 'coasting', and even of intelligent falling—all these were subjects that received much attention in the manuals, and might, in some cases, require years to master. Upright posture and skill in 'ankling' were generally regarded as the hallmarks of real expertise.

To celebrate a new edition of Sturmey's *Indispensable Handbook*, on 1 October 1887 *Punch* printed 'Ye Bicyclists of England' in four verses. The first three of these ran:

> Ye Bicyclists of England
>> Who stride your wheels with ease,
> How little do you think upon
>> What Mr Sturmey sees.
> The wheelman's standard rises high
>> With every year that goes.
> Wheels sweep, fast and cheap
>> Whereof Sturmey's trumpet blows—
> Our cycles range more swift and strong,
>> And Sturmey's trumpet blows.
>
> The cycles of our Fathers
>> Were 'boneshakers' and few,

But the cinder-path's broad field of famè
    Shows what their sons can do.
When Wyndham* rose, and Stanton fell,
    The pace was cramped and slow;
Their creep to our sweep
    Rouses Sturmey's scorn, you know—
Our cycles now run fleet and strong,
    And Sturmey's trumpets blow.

Britannia needs no bulwark—
    Tariffs her trade to keep,
Her 'wheels' are found on every path;
    Coventry's not asleep.
Our Woods and Howells wheel like fun,
    Jack Keen can make 'em go.
Foes we floor from each shore,
    Whereof Sturmey's trumpets blow—
Our cyclists lick the world by long,
    And Sturmey's trumpets blow.

* Wadham Wyndham, of London BC, Amateur Champion, 1877.

The first and greatest ride round the world by a cyclist was successfully undertaken on an Ordinary by an American riding an American machine. Thomas Stevens, a young reporter of Massachusetts, set off on a 'Columbia' 50in wheeler, made by the Pope Manufacturing Company, from San Francisco on 22 April 1884. He arrived on it at Yokohama, to board the Pacific mail steamer for San Francisco, on 17 December 1886. He had crossed America, Europe, Asia, by road, track, camel trail or water course, 'not merely a man perched on a lofty wheel, as if riding on a soap bubble, but also a perpetual object lesson in what Oliver Wendell Holmes calls "genuine, solid, old Teutonic pluck" '.

Stevens fitted out the 'Columbia'—of which models, selling for about $135, were available in seven sizes of front wheel, from 47in to 59in, two sizes of rear wheel, 16in or 18in, weight about 36lb—with a Butcher spoke cyclometer, and carried spare spokes, a cake of 'fire cement' for his red rubber tyres, an extra 'tire' for the rear wheel (wrapped round the front axle along with twenty yards of small stout rope), a bottle of sewing-machine oil, a suit of 'gossamer rubber', and his sundries in a Lamson carrier. A 'bicycle camera' and paper negatives were sent out to him via Calcutta.

This 'wheelman', as he calls himself, apart from a header in a sand-hole in North Turkey with 'a fearful shaking up', a few brushes with marauders—on occasion he could show a clean pair of heels to horsemen in pursuit—and the persistent prying and demands for endless riding displays by all and sundry, made light of his astounding performance. From Liverpool, on the European leg of his journey, he was given a send-off by members of the Anfield Club. The smooth macadam of the Lancashire-Cheshire roads delighted him: his comment on England was that it was 'a natural paradise of Cyclers'. When benighted in eastern deserts or mountain country he up-ended his machine, used the big wheel as frame and his 'gossamer' as tent cover and lighted a fire to keep off stray animals at the entrance. The Mayor of Angora (Ankara) remarked: 'The next thing we shall see will be Englishmen crossing over to India in balloons and dropping down to Angora for refreshment'. From Constantinople on to India Thomas Stevens covered very much the same route as that the writer recently traversed by overland bus: even in the conditions met with today he would earn ungrudging admiration.

CHAPTER FOUR

XTRA-ORDINARIES
AND OTHERS

THE APPEAL of the Ordinary, whatever the enthusiasm it kindled among athletic young men and the spectators at some of the big meets and championship events, was limited. The main cause of this, apart from the cost of a good machine, was its lack of stability, both lateral and, more especially, fore-and-aft. Headers or 'imperial crowners' were ever-present possibilities not lightly supported by all would-be enjoyers of the new mode of private transport. To be perched six feet above the ground, with pedals flying round as the rider dangled his legs over the handlebars to 'coast' a downhill stretch, looked dashing, but with a loose stone, loose tyre, stray dog or hen it could be disastrous. The advice when the machine ran away with one to 'steer for the nearest hedge and choose a soft spot to land on', if practical was none the less intimidating.

On the race track the high machine was spectacular and graceful. Those who rode it most successfully were tall, powerful men with a long reach of leg; many of the early champions—Keith Falconer and J. S. Whatton of Cambridge BC, Cortis, F. J. Osmond of Norwood, H. Synyer of Nottingham, R. H. English of North Shields —all stood over six feet in their stockings. They were the natural aristocracy of the racing path. But the average rider of average height felt the disadvantage. His turn was to come with the 'safety', when the shortest man was on equality with the tallest. 'Safety' cracks were usually of a different breed from 'ordinary' riders, not long of limb but stocky and muscular.

Various attempts, therefore, were made from the late seventies to make the Ordinary safer, and at the same time there were approaches to the problem of bicycle design from an altogether different direction.

One means of reducing the danger of a header was to have the rider of an Ordinary seated farther back instead of so directly over the pedals. At the suggestion of an amateur cyclist from Weymouth a 50in Xtra-Ordinary Challenge was made by Singers of Coventry, patented in October 1878 (see plate, p36). It had the steering head in line with the point of contact with the wheel and the ground, which greatly assisted control, the front forks raked considerably backwards, and a system of linkage levers used for the pedals, since the rider could not have reached them now if placed on the front axle. For additional comfort and security the pedals were rubber-studded. The 'Xtra' weighed 54lb and, although designed for safety rather than speed, covered a road distance of 10 miles in 35min 47sec when ridden by a professional. Its disadvantage has been noted above by Rumney.

Some idea of the engineering precision that went into a Singers' 'Challenge' may be entertained from the description of one of these machines that was rescued from a rubbish heap of discarded bedsteads, bicycles and motor cars some eighty years later, and lovingly resurrected. Its direct spokes radiated from solid bronze-flange hubs carried on a forged steel spindle, the ends of which were housed in a double circle of steel ball-bearings running in cups of polished steel. The whole was enclosed in a housing on which the name W. Bowns, Birmingham—'Aeolus patent adjustable bearings'—could be seen. Finger-tip adjustment could be effected and secured by a locking device. The pedals, of special design, were set on adjustable cranks, fixed to the ends of the spindle by cotters and locking nuts, the whole assembly being finished in heavy nickel plate. The driving wheel was mounted between forks of very slender proportion, shaped in fish-back style to lessen wind resistance, hollow yet strong. In the head were concealed hardened steel pivots to provide smooth steering movement: this was controlled by handlebars of generous width with buffalo horn handlegrips.

The 'Challenge' had a spoon-type brake operated by a spring-loaded handle and applied direct on to the rubber-tyred wheel. The frame or backbone was made from hollow steel tubing of oval section, closely following the contour of the driving wheel. Its rear end terminated in a carefully forged fork to carry the small rear wheel. The saddle, of real leather, was placed so as to allow maximum leg reach to the pedals, and tucked in behind was a small tool pouch. Apart from all the bright parts, which were nickel-plated, the machine was finished in black japan. The rescuer of this machine was able to identify it as one of the models manufactured in 1886.

Similar in principle and appearing in the same year, the 'Facile' bicycle patented by John Beale and manufactured by Ellis & Company, London, was a popular and successful alternative. A front wheel somewhat smaller, at most 48in, a saddle placed well back, raked forks and pedals connected by links to the cranks, with a weight of 43lb—everything recommended it as a club machine. The makers organised races for 'Faciles' only—no small aid to their commercial success—and in a 24hr event in 1883, J. H. Adams covered 221¼ miles. A year later the same rider beat the Land's End to John o' Groats record on a 'Facile', bringing the time down to within seven days. With a racing model geared 'Facile', introduced in 1887, weighing only 37¼ lb, and with ball-bearings throughout and sun-and-planet gearing, another rider, F. W. Shorland, covered the distance from London to Brighton and back in 7hr 19min. In doing so he beat for the first time the coaching record, 7hr 50min, which had been established with the aid of sixty-four horses, incidentally bringing to pass also the 'hobbyhorse' prophecy (p15). Shorland's time for the London-Edinburgh run (44hr 49min) lopped no less than ten hours off the previous best. Yet again, entering for the prize offered by the makers for the first rider of one of their machines to achieve 300 miles in 24hr, P. A. Nix of the Brixton Ramblers BC achieved 297 miles on the geared 'Facile', which was accepted as qualifying for the prize—a new bicycle, a diamond ring and a gold medal.

Whereas the 'Xtra' and the 'Facile' were fairly orthodox variations upon the Ordinary, the American 'Star' boldly took the bull by the horns. Made first by G. W. Pressey of Hammonton, New Jersey, under a patent of 1880, then in more practical and successful form by the H. B. Smith Company of Burlington, New Jersey, to a design patented in 1885 by W. S. Kelley, the 'Star' had its large wheel at the rear and small at the front. It was driven by means of two ratchet and pawl clutches on each side of the rear wheel. Depressing the pedal caused the drum to revolve, and as a pawl on the wheel spindle engaged with a ratchet tooth inside, so the road wheel was rotated. As in a pawl free-wheel the clutch went out of action on the pedal's upward stroke.

Somewhat daddy-long-legs like in appearance the 'Star' proved a notable racing machine in the USA. For starting, both pedals could be used at the top of the stroke and in a close finish an expert rider could 'jump' the bicycle by depressing them both together. An American cyclist brought the first 'Star' seen in England to the Harrogate 'camp' in 1885. Although serious consideration was given by Thomas Humber to obtaining English manufacturing

The American 'Star' racing machine

rights it was decided, after trials against an Ordinary, not to proceed here with the machine 'with its big front wheel at the back'.

The idea of reducing the diameter of the front wheel in the interests of safety, and at the same time employing some sort of gearing on it so that it might revolve faster than the pedals, occurred also to other English firms. 'A small wheel well-geared seems to be the coming favourite. The old objection [by high-wheel enthusiasts] that you are down where the dogs can reach you being balanced by the fact that you can more easily kick the canine' (*Wheeling*, November 1884). There was a front-driver safety, the 'Hall', made by Coupe, Addy & Hall of Sheffield, c 1880. Then at the Stanley Show, 1884, held at Covent Garden, the 'Kangaroo' dwarf bicycle came before the public. It had a 38in front wheel, geared to 56in, a 20in rear wheel and an adjustable riding position. It weighed 47½lb and cost 17 guineas. (Observers of the niceties of nomenclature preserve the term 'dwarf' for small or 'pony' front-driving Ordinaries—not necessarily safe or immune from 'headers'; 'safeties' generically covers all bicycles, high or low, which aim at safety; 'dwarf-safety' refers to rear-driven dwarfs.)

The firm that produced the 'Kangaroo', Hillman, Herbert & Cooper of Coventry, came to the cycle business in 1876. William Hillman, noticed above as associate of James Starley in the 'Ariel', had been a foreman at the Coventry Sewing Machine Company along with George Singer. For the 'Kangaroo' as for the 'Facile' a race was organised for advertisement purposes, and over a course of 100 miles George Smith beat all previous records with a time of 7hr 11min 10sec. In a second 'Kangaroo' race the following year the winner was Edward Hale—whose claim to real cycling fame is his subsequent feat of riding 100 miles every day, except Sunday, for a complete year. The attitude of 'dyed-in-the-wool' high-wheelers to these dwarf prodigies may be assumed from a comment on the Kangaroo in the *Wheel World*, as available 'for those who have the moral courage to face the British public on a safety bicycle', and by such rather sour comments as 'aided by one or two record performances, obtained by subsidizing the best known riders of the day over a particularly favourable course, this machine flashed into public notice like a meteor'.

Singers' 'Rational Ordinary', made as late as 1890, attempted to make a high bicycle safe, by the use of a larger heavier rear wheel as well as raked-back front forks. This permitted much less speed in comparison with the racers of almost vertical forks and very light back wheels, but in compensation 'headers' were also less likely. The spring and backbone were built open instead of closed, the tyres a full inch instead of ¾in, the rear wheel 24in or 26in high, and the driving wheel 'some inches less than the driver can stretch'. The machine could be safely ridden in rough conditions which would have brought the ordinary 'Ordinary' to grief at once. So road riders took to the 'Rational', racing men favoured the Crypto Cycle Company's geared Ordinary with a 49in driving wheel geared up to 62in or, a later development, the 'front driver' which had a 36in front wheel and hub with Crypto gearing.

On one of these 'front-drivers' weighing 32½lb the above-mentioned F. W. Shorland covered the record distance of 413 miles 1,615yd on the Herne Hill track in July 1892, in 24hr. Instead of cranks to drive the front wheel there was a pinion on the spindle and a ring of teeth on the inner circumference of the hub. Between the two a set of three small pinions revolved on studs mounted on the hub flange, giving the gearing up to 62in.

ON TRACK AND ROAD

Considerable changes, of course, had come about in cycle racing since early track days. Not only were the big men with their big wheels no longer assured of pre-eminence, but the tracks they had used were no longer adequate. Now special tracks existed, built with every regard for speed. The corners were carefully laid out and as much care bestowed on calculating the incline of the banking as would be given by a railway engineer to setting out a curve. The old-fashioned tracks had been those used by pedestrians : not only had they no banking, but often they sloped down to the outside edge. (Old-time professional riders had emulated the example of pedestrians and gone in for six-day contests or 'long wobbles', originally at the Agricultural Hall. An ex-collier, Waller, in 1879 accomplished a distance of 1,172 miles in the six days, after a first day's 253 miles.) A modern 'Safety' could not have been ridden round these tracks at anything like its top speed; probably not very much better times could have been made on such tracks as the old Lillie Bridge than were achieved on the old Ordinary. The amount of banking on modern race paths was such that when an ex-tricycle champion attempted to ride a three-wheeler round one at Olympia, he fell off on the inside for want of confidence, at first start, to take it at a sufficiently high speed.

Cycle tracks could be classified either as dirt tracks or those with cement or wooden surfaces. Cement was undoubtedly the material for propelling a machine at its fastest speed. The really good track was not only properly set out for its curves and banking, but had a surface that gave a proper grip to tyres, whether wet or dry. Those at Catford, Wood Green and Herne Hill were representative modern race paths, and there was a particularly fine track, with all facilities for both racing and training, at the Crystal Palace. The older one there, where Cortis first covered 20 miles inside the hour, had also been the best of its day.

In the provinces the old-time rider had to contend on and with such tracks as a gravel walk in the Horticultural Gardens, Leeds, with five laps to the mile, devoid of banking; or a cinder track at Halifax, three-and-a-half laps to the mile and almost round, so that high banks were regarded as unnecessary. Halifax, like Bradford, which could not offer a good track on which to train, failed to turn out good 'speed cyclers'. Bradford's remedy was to lay a wood track on Manningham football ground, if and when capital came available. To keep pace with the times Huddersfield decided to level their cricket ground and put down a cinder track, four laps to the mile, with easy corners, moderately banked and 30ft wide all round. As a result the most classic athletic meetings in the North of England, promoted there, found cyclists at no disadvantage. Previously they had been nearly 100yd slower per mile than such riders as F. J. Osmond, who made a record of 2min 28.5sec for the mile on the Paddington track in July 1890. (A contemporary track, made of concrete, with timber banking, at Central Park, San Francisco, tilted to an angle of $65\frac{1}{3}°$ at its turns, a rise of 13ft on a base of 21ft.) Leeds, at about the same time, laid down a new cycle track encircling the large cricket ground at Headingley, three laps to the mile, D-shaped, varying in width from 20 to 27ft, but with the drawback of being on the slope. Championship competitors resented the long drag of 160yd, but it provided the fastest half-mile track in the country 'seeing that for this distance the riders descend the hill twice'. There was accommodation for 25,000 spectators. Soon after this, because of 'a little difference a few cyclers had with the proprietors of the Headingley ground', a new athletic ground was formed with a 4 lap track banked on the most approved lines, dead level and nicely sheltered. Critics then were afraid that there was not room for two!

Short-distance path contests had also changed both in their nature and their results. In the days of Keen and Cooper the mile record had stood at $2\frac{3}{4}$ minutes. Within fifteen years it was to come down practically to even time, due partly to tracks and machines, but still more to the specialised form of pace-making. Pace-makers not only helped the 'crack' to maintain his speed, but afforded him substantial aid by cutting the wind and establishing a suction of air to ease his progress. To maintain a sufficient number of riders to pace any contest lasting over a distance was, of course, a most

68

expensive proceeding. Members of such crews expected both a standing salary and extra bonus for their efforts when the man they asisted broke a record. The favourite machines in use were the quadricycle, triplet or even quadruplet, and, to a lesser extent, the tandem. Pace-making was a regular art and to see the system on which such teams as the 'Gladiators' were organised was to understand the surprising nature of some results. As soon as one pacing implement had circled a few laps and its crew become tired, another came swooping along and, without a second being wasted, mechanically picked up the place previously occupied by the retiring crew.

The Americans went one better in the art after several attempts, on the Nashville track, to break existing records by creating a vacuum for the rider. To achieve a mile inside a minute they laid down a straight track inside a 4ft gauge railway line. A locomotive, drawing a special car carrying the time-keepers and other officials connected with the trial, did the pacing. The car was provided with a wind-screen extending down to within an inch of the track, and in the centre of the screen there was a white line for the rider to steer by. Half a mile was allowed to get up speed and the same distance to slow down, the middle distance of one mile being marked by 'torpedoes' or fog signals. The rider, Charley Murphy, followed the train at 60 mph with comparative ease and on one slight inequality in the track actually back-pedalled. From then on he was known as 'Mile-a-minute Murphy'. How different from the old procedure in scratch races and championships when riders had exercised scientific skill and 'used their heads' in the same way as a good jockey!

Remarkable times were made, also, on a half-mile track kept in perfect condition at the Springfield Diamond Tournament—so called because all the prizes were diamonds—regarded as the greatest of American race-meets. With a flying start, the favourite style in America, a mile inside 1min 55sec or even 1min 50sec was not beyond the bounds of possibility, early in the nineties. Most of the races here were for shorter distances than was usual in England, heats and races following each other rapidly with no 'loafing', so that the excitement was kept up and 'everyone went away delighted'.

Not all meets were as advanced or as 'gallery attracting' as this. A. W. Rumney, in his Cambridge days as club secretary, organised matches with other universities—if not Oxford, then with Dublin or Edinburgh. The first race for any kind of 'Safety', held in 1885, was 'really a menagerie affair' with one or two Kangaroos, a Sun and Planet (geared 'Facile') or two, and 'for comic relief' one rider mounted on an 'Xtra' (nicknamed the 'Camel'), and then Rumney himself on a 40in 'Pony' (an early dwarf built by the Coventry Machinists Company), 'whose pedals swung into the mud of the track and splashed everyone far and near,' since being fitted on secondary cranks at bottom they were only six inches above the ground. For club fixtures, runs up to a hundred miles, a small syndicate including Rumney purchased a sociable tricycle or 'club bus' where two riders sat side by side—perhaps a 'Club Sociable' from the Coventry Machinists Company with a Cheylesmore free-wheel clutch. (James Starley's contribution to the 'sociable' was that epoch-making device, differential gear. His 'Salvo' tricycle, 1877, was the first machine to be fitted with a bevel-gear differential unit, which enabled two riders pedalling independently to equalize their drive, and was so successful that at Queen Victoria's request two tricycles for royal use were delivered at Osborne House in 1881—'Royal Salvos'.) For serious racing Rumney bought a 56in club racer, 'a beautifully rigid machine with piano wire spokes', on the instalment principle. For touring solo he used first a 'Facile' Ordinary, then graduated to a cushion-tyred geared 'Facile', 'which was a little faster on the level but not such a good hill-climber'. Lacy Hillier, however, claimed that the Ordinary was faster on a rough surface and on the track for a final spurt.

70

Page 71 : Singer Cross-frame bicycle

Page 72 : Biggar Cycling Club, c 1890. Note the preponderance of cross-frame machines—the Ordinary was on the way out by this time

One sees this keen tourist with his 'Multum' ('*multum in parvo*' bag) fitted on the backbone and saddle, or his 'liver pad' (Sturmey's 'take-about', a mackintosh knapsack on a light cane-backed pad worn by the rider), with his Bartholomew's maps or Howard's *Roads of England and Wales*, which gave distances, hills and BTC hotels, setting off in green knickers and helmet from Keswick via Appleby and Aysgarth to the Harrogate camp. Or pushing against the wind from Brighton along the Portsmouth road en route for Stonehenge. Or 'paddling on', as 'Facile' riding was termed, into Scotland for Loch Lomond, Oban, Fort William and then back for the CTC meet at Edinburgh. After a long roasting day in the sun or in rain so persistent that he forwarded coat and baggage by train and rode in breeches and shirt in the rain-clouds, 'taking three hours over twenty-one miles on very bad road', he would take his ease at a CTC inn. (He does not disclose whether or not he carried as a change the recommended long pure wool combination garment, which completely clothes the body from neck to ankles in dry woollen attire, made by the Sanitary Woollen Company, Bradford.)

Proprietors of CTC houses entered into a contract with the club specifying that they would at all times receive and entertain any members who produced a valid ticket of membership and charge them the agreed tariff. One of Rumney's duties as a district consul was to keep a watchful eye on the tourist's comfort in his area. A standard tariff of the eighties was plain tea with eggs 1s 6d, or BTC tea (fish, ham and eggs, chop or steak) at 1s 9d or 2s, dinner 2s 6d, bed 2s, attendance charge 3d a meal and 6d for the chambermaid—based on the principle of commercial charges for the coffee room. And with luck there might be another chance-met enthusiast with whom to talk cycling in the commercial room 'till all was blue'.

The whole catalogue of items needed for a cyclist's outfit at this period bespeaks the dignity of the pursuit. It reads as follows:

E

	s	d
Jacket	32	0
Breeches or knickerbockers	16	0
Waistcoat	10	0
Shirt	11	6
Gaiters	8	6
Soft knockabout helmets	4	6
Helmets, any size	6	6
White straw hats, rough or smooth plait, with registered ribbon complete	4	6
Straw hats with ribbon	3	6
Registered ribbon without hat	2	0
Polo caps, ditto	2	9
Deerstalker or wideawake	5	9
Puggarees, for helmets	2	0
Cap covers	1	9
Stockings, any size	4	0
Gloves, any size	3	3
Silk handkerchiefs or mufflers, in club colours (grey checked ground, worked into amber and gold border), registered 24in square	6	6
30in ditto	9	0

The prices were those charged by the CTC and the advice was, for cycling clothing, to go to a practical cycling tailor 'who will appreciate the reason of the numerous little variations required from the regular model', such as woollen stiffeners, guaranteed all wool . . .

The last front-wheel driver was produced by Crypto Cycle Company in the mid-nineties and named the 'Bantam' (see plate, p53). '*Sans chaine, sans gêne*' it weighed less than 30lb, had almost vertical front forks but a forward-raked seat tube, which gave it a most business-like appearance: 'quite safe, easily learned, no step needed, very light, very fast, no stooping, no chain'. It was A. J. Balfour's favourite machine. Long before that time, however, 'Bantam' and dwarf bicycles of 'Kangaroo' style had received a challenge which, while not taking them out of the market or by any means reducing them to the scrap heap, spelt their progressive obsolescence. Most of the basic accessories, apart from pneumatic tyres and variable speed gear, had been evolved by 1880 and put to use on these 'Xtra-Ordinaries' and front-drivers, but, as even the Crypto's and Bantam's protagonists were compelled to admit, it was the chain-driven, rear-driving bicycle which became universal.

From the seventies onwards the bicycle had made good as a machine for the clubman tourist, the athlete, the sportsman— generally young men of the middle class. It had provoked amusement, admiration, ridicule and opposition. It had given Mr Punch opportunity for a 'Dumb Crambo' skit on the 'Sigh-cling Union' (figures of Romeo and Juliet), rubber tires (whist players), 'Boneshakers' etc (negro entertainers), and for a joke or two: Scottish wife (to her gossip), 'Ah dinna ken what's come ower the kirk. Ah canna bide to see oor Minister spankin' aboot on yon Cyclopaedy.' It had challenged the law and the interest and tolerance of the general public in abusing its free use of the highways. For during summer months there was race after race at various distances promoted by various organisations on the public roads—often in the London district, such as the 'fifty mile road ride' (so called to disguise its nature) from Hounslow to Cookham and back, or the London BC's Bath to London, 'kept very quiet but always excites interest'.

In the face of generally mounting hostility to the nuisance caused by a relatively small section of cyclists, attempts were made to brave it out by certain race managers. The police intervened and the 'home mile' of a fifty-mile 'ride' in September 1883 was blocked —in spite of the course having been deliberately changed just before the race. Notice was served that, under the Highway and

Metropolitan Police Acts, bicycles and tricycles were carriages, and a penalty could be imposed on any person riding or driving furiously or to the common danger of passengers in any thoroughfare. The 'road ride' was discontinued. In the interest of the future of organised cycling the NCU—the Jockey Club of cycling—came out against road races, and, in 1888, decided to confine its activities to the track. The later substitute, a means of getting round 'massed start' provocation, was to be the 'time trial'. But by that time the involvement of the public in bicycling was itself of a different order.

CHAPTER FIVE

FASHION AND HER BICYCLE: THE SAFETY

BEFORE QUEEN VICTORIA died the bicycle had become an established part of national life. As the first half of her reign produced the cheapening of public means of transport in the railway system, so the latter half saw the cheapening of private means of transport, the safety bicycle. Its general acceptance had far-reaching effects not only on the lives of men and women, but on the road system that would eventually see its replacement, as Everyman's form of transport, by the cheap car. While the boneshaker built by the village blacksmith had served to carry country labourers to work and postmen on their rounds (a few velocipedes were bought or hired by the GPO as an experiment), and while the Ordinary had supplied athletes and clubmen with hard exercise and adventurous touring, the Safety was to give Tom, Dick and Harriet, shop assistants and clerks, new freedom and chance to break out of their urban confines. But first it would have its season of high fashion and would cost somewhat more than a popular price.

In their day the term 'safety' was applied to those modifications

77

of the Ordinary described in the previous chapter. The short-sighted schoolboy, whose parents would only allow him to cycle on a safety (chapter 3) bought an Xtra 'Challenge' with a 50in wheel. Designs, however, which reduced the front wheel until it was equalised eventually with the rear, and also incorporated chain-driving to the rear wheel, gave the 'safety' bicycle its subsequent definitive form.

The earliest of these designs appeared in the *English Mechanic* of 1869 for a rear-wheel chain-driven bicycle as conceived by F. W. Shearing. Whether it was ever patented, much less built, is doubtful. The machine on the same principle made by George Shergold of Gloucester, some seven years later, was probably the first actually built in Britain: a closely contemporary Safety, by Rousseau of Marseilles, had its chain-drive to the front wheel. (Doubt surrounds the claim that the firm of Meyer, Paris, built a rear-wheel chain-driven bicycle, with wire-spoked, rubber-tyred wheels, for André Guilmet as early as 1869. What happened to it?) Shergold's machine survives still in the London Science Museum. It has a 29in front and 32in rear wheel, indirect steering with coupling rods between handlebars and steering head, a geared-up chain drive and an unusual S-shaped backbone frame. As this is the one example known to have been built, Shergold's Safety, like its rear-driven predecessor Macmillan's boneshaker, did not make a widely felt impression.

There were a number of other evanescent rear-driven machines but the first of the chain-driven Safety models to reach the public in any quantity was that exhibited at the Stanley Show, 1880, by the Tangent Bicycle Company from a patent design taken out by H. J. Lawson the previous year. (Lawson became manager of the firm on its amalgamation with Rudge's of Wolverhampton as the 'Rudge Cycle Company'.) The Lawson chain-driven Bicyclette—unofficially 'The Crocodile'—still had unequal wheels, front 40in, rear 24in, a straight backbone frame, 'bridle-rod' steering (indirect, through coupling rods from the handle to the front fork), with pedals and chain-wheel at the end of a vertical rod descending from the backbone. Its silhouette was not unlike its soubriquet. Its popularity was short-lived, but it was a landmark and it earned Lawson an engraved gold watch from the firm and subsequent glorification as 'inventor of the Safety bicycle'. Lawson had previously registered the word 'safety' for a rear-wheel lever-driven bicycle, weighing 65½lb, in which both hands and feet were used. He followed up his 'Bicyclette' (the term used in France to distinguish rear-driven dwarf from high Ordinary) with a Ladies' Safety (1884), a more practical machine.

In that year Lawson approached the Birmingham Small Arms Company (founded 1861), which had entered the cycle industry just four years before, and manufactured the Otto 'dicycle'—intended to supersede all bicycles and tricycles—with the proposition that they should manufacture his Safety Bicyclette. Two specimens were made, but during Lawson's delay in taking delivery BSA designed a Safety of their own, using rifle cleaning rods and tricycle parts where suitable to cut down expense. Their first BSA Safety, with 32in rear, 20in front wheel and indirect steering, cost £9 9s and achieved sales of more than 1,500 models. The following year BSA started to manufacture ball-bearings, but after 1888 the company went out of cycle manufacture and concentrated again on small arms—a phase which, apart from production of certain bicycle components, was to last another twenty years.

Other rear-drivers, notably a lady's model built by J. McCammon with single-tube drop frame and direct steering, and a Humber with an elementary form of diamond frame, but bearing a residual resemblance to the American 'Star', entered the dwarf market of the early eighties: both had rear wheels larger than the front. But it was John Kemp Starley's 'Rover' (nephew of James Starley) which achieved the breakthrough to popularity for this type of machine, and which, in its final design, was recognisably the predecessor of the modern safety bicycle.

J. K. Starley, after experience as a mechanic in Haynes & Jefferies' cycle works, had started out on his own in about 1878; soon after he took a partner, William Sutton. The first 'Rover' safety was evolved in 1884, a machine having the unhandy characteristics of its rivals—different sized wheels and indirect steering. It was exhibited at the Stanley Show, February 1885, and priced £22. A year later the firm of Starley & Sutton produced a modified version with a raked steering head and direct steering instead of 'bridle rods', weighing 37lb. It might have been overlooked as 'just another dwarf'—influential cycling champions like Lacy Hillier were still convinced of the Ordinary's superior capabilities—but in September 1885 a race over the distance of 100 miles was held for 'Rover' riders. The winner, George Smith again, broke the previous world record with a time of 7hr 5min 16sec, regaining the record from the 'Kangaroo', and in the same race the fifty-mile record was broken also. Publicity of that sort works wonders. Safety bicycle it might be, but, as the manufacturers claimed in their advertisements, it was also a speed model. (This riding by so-called amateurs of a particular maker's machine for a subsidy, often much more than the open professional earned, 'shamateurism', became a great scandal in the eighties. In France makers also spent large sums to maintain racing men to push the merits of their cycles, but they were open professionals with their patron's name printed boldly across their racing jerseys.)

As yet the 'Rover' had a backbone frame and unequal-sized wheels. It was the third model, with equal-sized wheels and diamond frame, though with two curved members and no stay between saddle and crank bracket, which set the pattern on which most manufacturers from then on were to base their designs and variations. The one element lacking to complete, in general style, a prototype of the standard modern bicycle, was the appropriate tyre.

So far solid rubber had served to dull the jarring progress of a bicycle ridden over most English roads—supported by a variety of spring saddles (the Arab 'cradle spring' of 1879 proved most adaptable), spring frames, spring wheels or 'anti-vibration handles'. Such tyres were narrow, usually ¾in or ½in for racing, and often came loose. The degree of comfort was probably less on the small-wheeled Safety than on the Ordinary. Hollow, non-inflatable thicker 'cushion' tyres were tried for a time—they were a 'luxury' fitted to the 'geared Facile' ridden by Rumney in 1890—but the real answer came only when the pneumatic tyre, re-invented and patented by J. B. Dunlop in 1898, became generally available.

Dunlop, the lowland Scot, was now a veterinary surgeon in Belfast, and produced the tyre for use in the first instance on his son's bicycle; it was taken up by Harvey du Cros and the Pneumatic Tyre Company formed. The tyre consisted of an inner tube and outer cover or 'tread' secured to the rim of the wheel by cementing and binding. At first it was costly and, as Rumney comments, 'very troublesome to repair being bandaged on to the rims', but within a year or two this 'sausage' tyre was being fitted to most Safety bicycles and to some Ordinaries as well. It was obviously more efficient than other anti-vibrator devices, intercepting road shocks before they reached the rim. Its effect on pace was demonstrated in May 1889, when, in the first race, in Ireland, in which pneumatic tyres were used, W. Hume of Belfast Cruisers CC beat very strong opposition on Ordinaries—and continued to do so in England. The 2in inflated tyres were, of course, ridiculed until they beat the ½in solids, and they were not exactly welcomed by those manufacturers who had to discard former models and produce new frames with forks wide enough to take the new tyres. By 1893 the price of a pair of Dunlops was still from £3 to £6 above the price of the old small solids, but a number of pirate tyres were also made, in Bristol, and factors sold wires, canvas and rubber treads separately to avoid proceedings. André and Edouard Michelin took out their patent, for pneumatic tyres with beaded edges, secured on the wheel rims by rings, in 1892. The detachable wired-on type of Dunlop was invented by C. K. Welch.

The public now had offered to them both safety and comfort. By 1893, although he was still faithful to the front-driver 'Facile', Rumney too had taken to a pneumatic for his 500 mile fortnight's tour in northern Ireland. Within another year or two solid and cushion tyres were virtually 'out'.

Starley's 'Rover' was to set the general pattern of cycle construction for almost another seventy years. But in the latter half of the 1880s and nineties there were also successful experiments with several other frame designs, and with other methods of transmission. To take the latter first, the 'Quadrant' chainless bicycle (1898) employed a Lloyd cross-roller gear and had a back-pedalling handbrake: but its shaft-drive transmission was not to prevail against the then established roller-chain drive. As to frame design the 'spring-framed' Safety, made by Linley & Biggs, Clerkenwell Road, London, was patented in 1885. In this machine, 'the Whippet', saddle, pedals and handlebar were all on a sprung sub-frame, separated from the main frame which carried the wheels by a strong coil spring and a moveable shackle in the steering. On a 'Whippet' with cushion tyres the 24 hours' road record was put up to 336½ miles by M. A. Holbein, 1890 (advanced to 361¾m the following year on a 'Swift' Safety) whilst between 1881 and 1891 three open hill climb events were won by a cycle-engineer employee of Linley's, W. Chater Lea. A 'spring-frame' bicycle produced by Cooper, Kitchen & Company, c 1888, had a diamond frame and more orthodox lines: there was a spring-frame 'Rover' as ridden by Viscount Bury, president of the NCU, and also a neater-looking British 'Star'. 'Whippets' enjoyed their period of popularity, though it was short-lived in face of the competition by pneumatic tyres.

Another variant style, the 'Cross-frame', employed by a number

82

of Safety manufacturers, including Rudge & Singers, has lately been revived after its long period of obsolescence. An outstandingly successful model was the 'Ivel' racing bicycle made by an agricultural engineer, Dan Albone of Biggleswade, and introduced in 1886. It was the first 'dwarf' that could be ridden without a tight hold on the handlebars or without any hold at all, as could Ordinaries. (Albone and A. J. 'Faed' Wilson also produced the first practical tandem bicycle with connected steering.) The output of these 'cross-frames', in which G. P. Mills of Anfield BC was associated, remained small but their reputations grew as racing enthusiasts took up the 'Ivel'. Mills himself beat the 50 mile road record on one, in 1888, with a time of 2hr 47min 36 sec. By replacing the straight front tube with a curved tube from the head to the bracket and adding a leather dress-guard secured to the chain-stay, Albone adapted the 'Ivel' as a ladies' machine the following year. Another cross-frame, high-priced but popular, the 'Featherweight', produced by the Centaur Company, Coventry (founded 1876), had a successor, the 'Featherbed' (1908) with 2in cross-section tyres, so anticipating the modern 'balloon' tyre. The same company produced the 'Ostrich', a safety of high-frame pattern and a 'King and Queen of Scorchers', the latter weighing 30lb complete with dress-guard.

As for racing style in these challenging days, Hewitt Griffin, of the London Athletic Club, gives illuminating hints in the 'All England Series' *Cycling* volume of 1890:

A graceful attitude on a Safety, when racing, is almost an impossibility, and old race goers may well sigh for the style in which such riders as Lt Byng and Jack Keen sat their machines. The first amateur champion, H. P. Whiting, was one of the introducers of the 'grasshopper' style of leaning over, which is almost imperative on the latter-day dwarf bicycles. The very latest fad of Safetyists is to get the saddle back as far as possible, so the position is still more like that on the bone-shakers, and riders rely more on the forward push than the downward thrust. Bad habits are easily acquired, and, as rider improves, he should strive to attain style as well as speed, and above all never stoop and wag the head. If, owing to the exertion, the shoulders are dropped, the head must be kept up and held still; it neither adds to the speed, nor does it impress the spectators, for a man to put out his tongue and wag his head like a china mandarin.

As for the new style of racing man, a pen portrait of Montague H. Holbein supplies hints:

This newly developed road demon is considered by the cognoscenti to be a phenomenally good man, destined to excel the form of even Mills and Hale. He is a native of London, stands about five feet ten, weighs 11st 9lb, with a well-knit figure, lithe and compact; possesses none of the bumptious, ill-bred tone too frequently associated with crack wheelmen, but is a gentlemanly man, courteous withal, but very talkative. His hair is black and his face is dark to swarthiness: and when heated and dusty from a long ride he looks like a mulatto.

WOMEN AWHEEL

Ladies so far had been tricyclists rather than bicyclists, both in this country and in America. *Harper's Weekly*, July 1886, portrayed couples on 'sociables' and open-fronted machines 'wheeling' on Riverside Drive. The tricycle, though heavy—90-110lb—was their choice for decency as well as for safety and comfort, in the era of the Ordinary. It might be a 'sociable'; an 'open-fronted' machine with two large front wheels and a single small rear one; a Humber 'Cripper' (so called from its first rider R. Cripps), with two large rear wheels and 20in pilot wheel, with bicycle steering; a Rudge 'rotary' with its large wheel on one side and two small ones on the other (developed from James Starley's Coventry Lever tricycle, the first modern tricycle, 1877); an Olympia rear-driven tandem tricycle; an 'Excelsior' one-two-three with all wheels of different sizes driven by wheel gear—or any one of a large number of both two-seater models or 'twicers', and single-seater models.

In 1887/8 alone fifty-seven patents for tricycles were granted and in the mid-eighties tricycles outnumbered bicycles at the annual cycle shows: in *Tricycles of the Year* (1884) 220 distinct machines were described. One of *Punch's* 'Illustrations to the Poets' in 1887 shows a pig-tailed Chinese pedalling a tricycle—'a Cycle of Cathay' (from Tennyson's 'Locksley Hall'). There were variants for the less active, such as the Coventry Chair, a passenger tricycle, and, for export, the 'Coolie Cycle', a tricycle made by the Coventry Machinists Company, fitted with a seat and footboard in front, saddle and pedals behind for the 'conductor' of the machine. There were also attachments to convert single tricycles into tandems. As a contemporary put it: 'The tandem tricycle will always be a popular mount, as the expert rider can thereon take a complete novice—his sister, his cousin or even in an emergency a lady who is not a relation.'

In country places dear old ladies in ankle-length tweeds can still sometimes be seen about quiet summery lanes on single tricycles of ninetyish appearance—by which period the machine had achieved its final form: direct steering, two-wheeled axle and a drive-through differential gear. This is not to disparage, of course, the Tricycle Association and its members, who can be seen about the roads today, in all weathers, on machines of modern trim.

But once the pneumatically improved Safety began to flood the market the tricycle's popularity as a tourer declined; and ladies, as well as gentlemen, could go it alone on two wheels. The beginning of bicycling was the end of the chaperon in England; 'now women, even young girls, ride alone or attended only by some casual man friend for miles together through deserted country roads' (*The Complete Cyclist*, 1897).

She still bestrides it, but how listlessly! A little while and she will suffer it to be wheeled into that *musée sentimentale* wherein she keeps, duly classified, specimens of her past foibles. . . . Already she has dropped it from her conversation; Rudge, Humber, Singer—she cares no longer to discriminate between machines which are, one and all of them, the devil's own patent.

Thus Max Beerbohm in an essay 'Fashion and Her Bicycle' collected into book form in 1899. The bicycle, in fact, had *arrived*—'all the world took to cycling,' says Rumney; 'the Upper Ten Disported themselves in Battersea Park'; had had its brief butterfly flight about 1895-7, and, as a craze, was beginning to fade out again. At its height *The Queen*, 'the Lady's Newspaper', May 1896, announced by way of rear-guard action :

> The Chaperon Cyclists Association has been formed under distinguished patronage to provide gentlewomen of good social position to conduct ladies on bicycle excursions and tours. . . . The chaperon provides her own cycle. The association is not responsible for accidents, but every reasonable precaution to prevent them will be taken.

But, argued Beerbohm, it made the lady ugly and ridiculous, 'for all the devices of her couturier Fashion never looked ought but her worst', and so, although its dullness and danger might be forgiven, it was soon bound to be dropped.

At its height, however, the voice from 'in' circles sounded otherwise. Mrs Harcourt Williamson wrote in *The Cycle in Society* :

> I have laid it down, as a rule, that only small women look their best upon wheels, but this, like every other rule, has brilliant exceptions. Few women ride more gracefully than Mrs W. H. Grenfell. I have seen her dressed all in soft green, a tweed skirt and velvet blouse, with gold belt and velvet Tam-o'-Shanter, looking more distinguished than anybody else as she passed through the throng in Hyde Park. At Battersea, which was always the most fashionable venue, Lady William Nevill and her tall husband were often seen riding together: and Lady William, always neat and well-dressed, looked her very best in navy blue, with a white sailor collar and cloth toque. Lady Minto, who bicycles nearly as well as she skates, and

Lady Griffin, who is also a very pretty rider, are both generally seen in navy blue and white, with sailor hats. . . . The whole secret of a woman looking well upon her bicycle lies in the cut and hang of her skirt. The very best skirt of all, in my opinion, is one made by Busvine, the great habit-maker, and made on the same lines as a habit, fitting the figure perfectly, and cunningly stretched and shrunk so to do . . .

Lady Archibald Campbell, an authority upon such subjects. has laid it down as a law that no costume can look equally well when walking and when upon wheels : but in speaking of cycling dress it is impossible to ignore the divided skirt. A young lady who took part in many of last season's musical rides looked particularly well, I remember, in one of these, which was made by Viola in grey Melton tweed. On the machine it looked particularly well, as it naturally fell into equal folds on each side of the wheels; and even walking quietly about one did not notice the division, which was only at the back, and hidden among the pleated folds. . . . The knickerbocker pure and simple is a very unbecoming style, the short full bags which are seen so often in the Bois de Boulogne being quite incompatible with elegance and grace; but I have seen women looking charming in these semi-manly garments when properly planned. Lady Eden, for instance, used to wear very long ones like Turkish trousers, 'soleil' pleated, and wearing them with a little bolero coat and broad belt she looked as feminine and charming as possible. Lady Augusta Fane, as good a bicyclist as she is a rider, has also worn a most becoming rational costume abroad. What can be done with grace abroad is almost impossible in England, and here I have never seen anybody really look well wearing anything but skirts.

Fashion is international. I treasure a coloured double-spread plate, supplement to *Vanity Fair*, 1897, in which the *haut ton* of French society and *grandes cocottes* are shown in the Bois de Boulogne all mounted on tandems and bicycles—Princess de Sagan, Princess and Prince de Broglie, Duchesse Doudeauville, Duchesse and Duc de Rohan, Comtesse Liane de Pougy, Comtesse Martel

(Gyp), Colonel Gibert, Coquelin Cadet, La Belle Otero and Cléo de Mérode. Evocative names and styles, with straw hats and veils, leg of mutton sleeves and frilled fronts! *Cycling World Illustrated* informed its readers that a young Parisian widow consoled herself in her bereavement by cycling in crape knickerbockers!

In Britain beauty and fashion were represented by such bicycle devotees as Ellen Terry (president of a club), Mrs Langtry (the 'Jersey Lily'), Sarah Bernhardt and all the royal princesses, while Miss Frances Willard, head of the temperance movement in America, declared her belief in it as 'a means of reformation for people upon whom the terrible drink crave has taken hold'. Miss Leila Woodhull and her mother even proposed on their next trip to America a cycling exploration of the Rocky Mountains.

It is amusing to note that, as in the twentieth-century love affair with the motor car, when a celebrated racing driver can say of his Ferrari, 'If I had a big enough front door, I'd take it in the house with me and up to bed', so in 1896/7

the bicycle has come to be so carefully considered that no menial is entrusted with the task of putting it into the guard's van when travelling about, and when at home it finds its home, not in the stables or any outbuildings, but in the hall itself. In the marble Hall of Chelsea House, in Londonderry House, in Grosvenor House, and other most palatial mansions, the bicycle stand is now a matter of course. . . . It is rather amusing to see a machine being wheeled along a platform snugly encased in its Crom-a-boo cover—a great protection from the scratches which so frequently disfigure a new coat of paint.

And as with the decor and upholstery of certain custom-built cars,

it is certainly the exception nowadays to see a bicycle with ordinary black or unembellished paint. Most women and many men have their machines painted in their own particular colours. Lady Archibald Campbell is generally dressed in drab,

Page 89 : Dursley-Pedersen

Page 90 : An Edwardian cyclist with a high machine

and her smart machine is painted to match. . . . Lady Huntingdon has her machine painted green with primrose lines upon
it; Miss Cornwallis West's colours are crimson and blue; Prin-
cesse Henry of Plessee has the prettiest white machine that ever
was seen; and no expense was spared in the finishing off of
General Stracey's machine, which is done in the well-known
red and blue of the Guards. [Mrs Harcourt Williamson.]

One of the notables who took up cycling and, whilst at Trinity,
Cambridge, won his half blue in competitive racing was the Hon
C. S. Rolls. He often steered a pacing triplet, came third in a four-
mile race at Herne Hill, 1896, and rode in a fifty-mile challenger
race organised by the CUBC the next year—thus doing something
to remedy *Cycling's* complaint: 'It is a plain bald fact that there
are very, very few racing men of what is generally known as good
social position.' Rolls was also fined the sum of 2s 6d and 2s costs
for riding a bicycle without lights. But in his last year at Cambridge
his Peugeot car took up his leisure, and, though incidentally,
Cycling reported from 'an authority on society matters' that the
cycling craze was at an end in London.

While it lasted as a status symbol the bicycle went everywhere :
to Ranelagh, to Sheen House, once a royal residence and then a
cycling club premises patronised by royalty, to 'musical rides' and
evening 'illuminated rides', where all lady riders wore white, to
gymkhanas, even on one occasion from Hatfield to the Foreign
Office, with despatches : and, of course, to Dieppe and Trouville.
On a more humdrum plane, this side of the Channel, the back-page
advertisement in the *CTC British Road Book* reiterates the trend :
'Follow the Fashion, set by Royalty, the Aristocracy and Society
and ride Rudge-Whitworth cycles, which are unrivalled for Speed,
Comfort, Safety and Strength.' All the royalties of Europe seem to
have patronised the sport, except the Emperor of Germany. Another advertisement, with a bicycle carrying a veiled and ankle-
length-costumed lady, reads : 'SWIFT cycles are high grade cycles :
write for a catalogue album, a work of art'. For the less well-heeled :

91

F

'Cycles of any make for Ladies, Gentlemen and Children may be purchased on the Gradual Payment system through any cycle agent in any part of the country: one twelfth part of the total required down and one twelfth part each month until all is paid'.

Much as some wished to believe that cycling might have been always confined to the comparatively few instead of being applied to the pleasure of the many, if it had not been 'taken up by the right people and straightway become the craze of the season', the evidence suggests otherwise. The idea that 'what once is approved by the classes will in the end be patronised by the masses', and that someone like Lady Norreys when she 'jumped lightly on to her machine, and, ringing her bell smartly once or twice as warning, wheeled away, with her dogs frisking and barking behind her' before an admiring little crowd in Great Cumberland Place, turned bicyclists from 'cads on castors' to exemplary members of society, is too good to be true.

Economics came into it where the many were concerned. An historian of the period, writing in 1897, makes special mention of the hold which cycling so soon obtained on the middle classes:

A favourite rendezvous in the neighbourhood of London is Bushey Park, and there when the weather is fine as many as a thousand bicyclists congregate. During the summer too, in the heart of the city, when the business traffic of the day is done and the streets are clear, an active scene may often be witnessed by gaslight. Under the shadow of the Bank and the Exchange, the asphalt thoroughfare is covered with a host of bicycle riders, performing a series of intricate evolutions on their iron steeds. [T. H. Escott]

The sisters and wives of doctors, lawyers, bankers, clergy etc, started to brave public opinion and take to the roads and suburban streets by themselves on comfortable pneumatic tyres. It was Society which adopted the idea—and no doubt encouraged the boom that soon built up. But the fashionable scene got the lion's share of reporters' attention, as usually happens.

92

Fashion and Her Bicycle : the Safety

It was on one of the dullest and most forbidding mornings of last month [January] that we mounted our safety and set out on what looked like the wildest of goose-chases, the review of the cycling world of fashion in Hyde Park. It was not until we had crossed the bridge, and had got fairly on the well-kept road that runs along North of the Serpentine, that we struck the main vein of the fashionable cycling crowd. Here, all the way up to the Achilles statue, where they turned and came back again, there was a constant and thick up-and-down stream of riders, all proceeding decorously and quietly, at a universal pace of eight miles an hour. All ages were represented, but chiefly young people; from the youngster of 12, with the usual propensity to indulge in sudden swooping curves, regardless of everything, to the grandfather of massive proportions and cautious movements on his trusty tricycle.

In all there must have been several hundred riders out on this raw and gloomy morning. . . . It was an animated, pretty and pleasing scene; the best of Society at their best. Stately fur-cloaked mammas watched their children and their elder daughters disport themselves with the new-found, health-giving pleasure; and young gallants, sometimes costumed in shooting habit, sometimes in short walking jacket, with trousers tightly strapped up at the ankles, but never in ordinary cycling clothes, rode with the ladies, and encouraged the half-fearful beginners to persevere.

At all events, the nation, which used to be divided into the equestrian and pedestrian orders, had now found a third rank, that of wheelmen and women. It was part of the social transformation of the Victorian age and was especially significant on the women's side. For when, in addition to pedestrians and carriage-folk, cyclists came into their own, for them an entirely new freedom and independence was implied.

Most lady riders probably *began* their cycling experience on sociables or tandems. 'On a tandem with a gentleman companion she looks most at home, as she flits by on the front seat, clad in a well-fitting costume' (but, unlike at home, unchaperoned). Once

93

she had been persuaded to try the rear-driving Safety, however, and had discovered that for riding it skill was more important than mere physical strength, the lady found the bicycle's advantages indisputable. It was lighter, simpler to mount, more graceful, capable of negotiating most roads on its single track and easier to stop : it was, for a time, the most popular—and the fastest—mode of private transport throughout the country. Women were following their urge towards emancipation : with their own clubs, the bicycle and tennis instead of croquet, they would go far towards becoming 'New Women'.

> The lady rider of the period was exhorted to cultivate an erect and alert, though easy carriage in the saddle : to learn to assist her pedalling by ankle action and to cultivate 'form' in riding. She must not spread her elbows abroad and turn out her toes : she must not hang forward over the handlebars, nor shuffle in the saddle. She must, in a word, eschew all awkward tricks and try to check the first tendency to a slovenly style of riding. [H. H. Griffin]

The magazine writers lost no opportunity of both rubbing in the lesson and suggesting its feminine allure :

> Neat ankle action is one of the chief points of graceful and expert riding. Don't sit like a stupid duck on the saddle and require the pedals to push up and down your limbs : raise the leg naturally when on the upward curve and learn to drive from the thighs with a clawing rather than a thrusting action. Remember that you have a most beautifully formed ankle, which separates the human foot from the clumsy appendages of the waddling tribes. Be worthy of this ankle and see that it enables you to ride well. [N. G. Bacon, *Our Girls Awheel*]

The same writer went on to expound the physical advantages and pleasures of 'our wheel'. Provided the cycle was used as a health preserver, and not as a health destroyer, the nerves were quickened, the energies awakened, the muscles rested, the circulation stimulated and a feeling of physical satisfaction throughout the system would ensure calm and invigorating sleep. In moderation cycling should strengthen the system : directly it was followed by loss of appetite, restlessness and sleeplessness, the limits of healthy cycling had clearly been exceeded. It was important also to preserve the equilibrium of balance for enjoyable and beneficial cycling : if the saddle was either too high or too low, the handlebars too close or too far away or the pedals beyond comfortable reach, girls might receive injury, even lasting damage, to their immature forms. It was also inadvisable to get over-heated while riding : this was very injurious and might easily cause ill-health.

Dress, obviously, had a large share in temperature control. Costume for lady cyclists changed from the inconvenient ordinary wear of long skirts, tight jackets, homburg or straw hats, to 'rational'. 'To ride a bicycle properly is very like a love affair : chiefly it is a matter of faith. Believe you can do it and the thing is done : doubt and for the life of you, you cannot'; but to ride it effectively and comfortably was a matter of common sense in dress. So while the young man in *Wheels of Chance*, the cycling tale which opens in H. G. Wells's Putney, August 1895, had his new brown cycling suit, a Norfolk jacket, knee breeches and thick chequered stockings, the young lady cyclist he encountered (mounted on a diamond-frame safety with Dunlops and a loofah-covered saddle) had a grey costume of 'rationals'.

Mr Punch, of course, as he was bound to do, found in them a source of humour. 'What a ridiculous costume!' says the lady cyclist, touring in north Holland, glancing at a bloused and baggy-trousered Dutchman : *'Nosce te ipsum'* (Know thyself) reads the caption. And to the fair bicyclists, the Ladies Rota and Ixiona Bykewell, whom he meets in stockings, knickerbockers and long-belted jackets at the church porch, the vicar remarks : 'It is customary for men, I will not say Gentlemen, to remove their hats on entering church.' Ridiculous as rational costume appeared to the caricaturist, it was far less likely to provoke ridiculous situations

'Rationals'—practical attire for cycling—from
H. G. Wells' Wheels of Chance (1895)

than dragging skirts covered with mud or caught up in the chain, or weighted with shot sewn into the lower edge, even fastened to the front of the boots or shoes, in an effort to prevent it riding up over the knees. Of the young lady in grey, her machine could not have cost much under £20, Wells's draper-hero speculated: 'Probably she was one of these here New Women. He had a persuasion the cult had been maligned. Anyhow she was a lady. And rich people, too! His mind came round and dwelt on her visible self. Rational dress didn't look a bit unwomanly.'

The cycling dress for ladies, as recommended by the CTC about this period and 'perfected by active riders in constant work', comprised the following:

A combination merino or woollen garment to be worn next to the body.

A pair of dark grey woollen or merino stockings.

A pair of loose knickerbockers fastened with elastic, or by a cloth strap and buckle, under the knee.

A pair of trousers cut loose to just below the knee, and thence tighter just down to the foot.

A plain skirt without kilting, and of sufficient fullness to admit of absolute freedom of movement without undue bulk.

A bodice or jacket cut either to fit the figure, or of 'Norfolk' shape, lined throughout (including sleeves) with flannel.

A helmet or hat of cloth or of straw, with a special and registered ribbon.

A pair of soft 'Tilbury'd' doeskin gloves.

The outfit should not be 'too thick or too heavy and neither too light nor too dark in colour', but a heavy grey medium. Wool and flannel were of great moment 'as the danger of colds is possibly greater with those who do not so frequently indulge in exercise', and it was additionally noted that all-wool corsets were now obtainable, so removing 'a drawback that has existed for some time in this connection'. Lady riders, however, who meant to ride in earnest and not play at cycling, were warned to avoid a tight-fitting bodice which, 'however well it may look, must of necessity be hot and uncomfortable'.

ON TOUR

H. G. Wells himself moved from Putney to Woking, where he and his wife could 'learn to ride bicycles and restore our broken contact with the open air'. He rode wherever the hero of *Wheels of Chance* rode, on a diamond-frame machine, with an uncertain plunger brake (though, in fact, the Foley back-pedal brake or pneumatic cycle brake were available by this time) and no free wheel, 'so that you could only stop and jump off when the treadle was at its lowest point'. Then his wife and he wandered about the south of England very agreeably on a 'tandem bicycle of a peculiar shape made by the Humber people'. (Humbers, who in 1890 brought in one of the best Safeties, the first really modern diamond frame, also produced in 1891 a diamond-frame bicycle with several improved features and a new, unique design of steering-head.) His comment on road conditions there shows the attraction for the townsman of this new chance to see something of the country in the days when 'there were no automobiles and the cyclist had a lordliness, a sense of masterful adventure, that has gone from him altogether now.' There was a chance, undisturbed, to notice the scenery and to botanise : miles of pinewood and oak forest, purple, heathery moorland and grassy downs stretched before him with purple vetch in the hedges, meadowsweet, honeysuckle, stellaria, traveller's joy, bedstraw, white campion, ragged robins and belated brambles.... There were no chemical sprays in 1895. Traffic consists of a milk chariot rattling by, a fruiterer's van, a man on horseback, a sluggish cartload of bricks, and another 'glittering wheel', which proves to be 'a working man riding to destruction on a very tall Ordinary'. (The working man was generally one stage behind : a rickety boneshaker rider in the Ordinary era, a second-hand Ordinary rider among the Safeties.)

Wells's early novels—*Wheels of Chance* (a cycling classic), *Kipps* and *Mr Polly*—are full of bicycles and the flavour they imparted to that age. In the first there is a splendid chase of Hoop-driver and Jessie by a clergyman ('We are all cyclists nowadays') on a tricycle of antiquated pattern with two large wheels in front, a highly-geared tandem bicycle with 'fat pneumatics' that nothing could beat downhill, and the massive bulk of a Marlborough Club tandem tricycle 'conspicuously secondhand', with all the usual Wellsian humours and occasional disregard for discrepancies in detail. As to the fugitive Jessie who, discontented at home and having read books 'about being free and living our own life and all that kind of thing', had taken to her bicycle to elope, her school-mistress remarks, 'I can only ascribe your action to that spirit of unrest that has seized so many women in these busily idle Latter Days.' In *Kipps* one meets the immortal Chitterlow—'It's curious how one runs up against people at bicycling.'

How cheerfully the wheels buzzed in that era when 'The world is divided into two classes: those who ride bicycles and those who don't.' Like the nonsense chorus of 'Ta-ra-ra-boom-de-ay' sung by Lottie Collins, which affected the country like an epidemic from 1892-6 and seemed to give expression to the new-found freedom—the 'Ca ira' of a generation—the bicycle and the woman cyclist were the visible signs of freedom.

The new joys of the open road were very real ones. Visitors to England took to them with enthusiasm. A sketch in the *Illustrated London News*, July 1898, shows a mixed party of American cyclists skimming happily along quiet village lanes with the impedimenta of the tourists—acetylene lamp, satchel and camera. (Among the machines which had greatly increased the popularity of the bicycle in the USA and helped to make cycling a social recreation as well as a sport and a means of transport, was the Overman Wheel Company's 'Victoria' drop-frame model for women—invented so that the rider could sit astride without having skirt trouble with the crossbar—and the 'Columbia' double drop-frame, with small gusset plates connecting the bars for added strength). Now, as a side effect,

99

those inns and travellers' hotels which had fallen into sleepiness and decay when the railways supplanted coaches, revived and flourished again as cyclists began to come in droves. Even the more splendid and exclusive hotels went out of their way to offer facilities: the Queen's, the largest hotel in Keswick, was a CTC headquarters; Pitlochry and Strathpeffer hydros advertised cycle accommodation, and the latter added 'Cycle court with professional attendants' to the catalogue of its amenities.

At the end of this progressive century there was revealed, by the 1901 census report, an increase over the last decade of forty-five per cent in the number of vehicle-makers—clearly indicating the rise to wide popularity of the bicycle. 'Motor-makers' were reported for the first time. The cycling craze reached its peak in the USA about 1899: there were then 312 factories operating night and day to produce an annual turnout of well over one million machines, an estimated five-fold increase within a decade. In addition, many American manufacturers opened depots in London to take advantage of the seller's market with their machines.

Membership of the CTC was increasing in the same period by up to 10,000 annually, and in 1899 reached a high-point, 60,449 members in the year of the club's majority. Its offices had moved from Newcastle to Bradford and then to London, Victoria Street. Among its aims, as set out in the *CTC British Road Book*, 1893, were to encourage and facilitate touring in all parts of the world; to provide riding or touring companions; to compile maps and road books specially adapted to the requirements of the cyclist; and to inculcate an *esprit de corps* in the brotherhood of the wheel, upholding and promoting the true interests of cycling the world over. With 'consuls' in every town to give information, official repairers and special-term hotels and inns, the touring cyclist felt he was in a privileged position. All this for an entrance fee of one shilling and an annual subscription of five shillings. If he chose he could set most of his anxieties on other shoulders when he set out for a week's or a fortnight's freedom awheel.

He could embark, as the writer's parents did in their early married days about the turn of the century, on cycling tours in France, visiting Paris and the Franco-British exhibition, without making too big a hole in their savings. Or, more ambitiously, like George, Harris and J. in *Three Men on the Bummel* (1900), he could envisage crossing to Hamburg, seeing Berlin and Dresden, then working a way to the Schwarzwald, through Nuremburg and Stuttgart. In Jerome K. Jerome's account of the subsequent trip there are many preliminary digs at the tandem v single bicycle controversy, at the 'patent gas' and the electric lamp, at the 'spiral' spring saddle or the divided one, constructed on anatomical principles, and at the so-called 'automatic' brake.

In their white flannel knickerbocker suits, however, the trio finally get off and reach the Black Forest. It is there, among the endless wooded hills, that they reflect more generally upon their mounts and the sport of bicycling. They compare the advertising poster's image with the actual performance. On a 'Bermondsey Company's Bottom Bracket Britain's Best' or a 'Camberwell Company's Jointless Eureka' or a 'Putney Popular' the rider generally shown is a lady, her sylph-like form poised airily on a luxurious saddle as she passes up hill and down hill, over road surfaces calculated to break the average steam roller—apparently with unseen heavenly aid. 'No fairy travelling on a summer cloud could take things more easily than does the bicycle girl', according to these posters. If it is a mere man he is riding 'on his pedals as he nears the top of some high hill to apostrophize the sun or address poetry to the surrounding scenery'. No cyclist, it seems, ever *works*. Or if he does, it is his own fault: he must be riding a machine of inferior make. (In this, of course, there was a grain of truth.) George, Harris and J. clearly have grounds for complaint: having bought the advertised brands of machine they are still left with all the work. But George's idea, to train up the hills and ride down

101

the hills is not very well received. It would not be playing the game.

The douche of Jerome's humour did not damp either rider's or maker's efforts. The cycle industry went in for a bout of over-capitalisation as financiers seized the opportunity of the boom. Riders, both on track and on the highway, enjoyed peak status. At cycle races, such as those held at the Crystal Palace, London attendances of twenty to thirty thousand watched professional riders, paced by quintet machines, make new Safety records. In the USA Charlie Millar, in 1898, covered over 2,093 miles in a six-day cycle race on a pneumatic-tyred Safety. (The first of such races took place in 1891 at Madison Square Gardens, New York, on high-wheelers.) Next year Marshall Taylor, aged 21, became the only negro ever to hold both the American and the world professional cycle racing championships. In the British Amateur Championships between 1897 and 1912 out of ninety events at distances from one-quarter to fifty miles, fifty-three were won on Rovers, descendants of those first machines described as having 'set the fashion to the world'.

For tourists there were all manner of guide books and maps to give good advice, cycling routes and warning of 'dangerous hills'. (There was no absolute definition of what constituted a 'dangerous hill'. The early criterion applied was the capability of an average rider on an Ordinary bicycle to descend steep declivities unknown to him—though they might be perfectly safe to descend on a Safety or a tricycle.) Maps, such as Bacon's *Cycling and Road Map of England and Wales*, showed such hills with one- or two-feathered 'danger' arrows beside the steep declivity. The road into Kendal from the west, for example, carried a two-feather arrow as did that from Thirsk to Helmsley at Sutton Bank; the road north from Sheffield to Barnsley carried one, as did that out of Durham towards Newcastle. Rumney, as chairman now of the CTC Map and Road Book Committee, made arrangements with

Bartholomews for a new series with strip map, profile and information in three parallel columns.

There were also 'Safety' cycling maps which showed the different classes of roads, difficult and dangerous hills and unrideable roads by distinct colourings—as well as the approximate speed over which each road could be travelled, and, compiled by the same Harry Inglis, *Contour Road Books*, which gave all routes in a series of diagrammatic road elevation plans, with descriptive notes and gradients. From Coventry to Hinckley, for example (1900), 'The main route is through Nuneaton, but that road is very bumpy and there are car lines. The best road is by Wolvey. Hinckley to Market Bosworth good surface. Nuneaton to Atherstone good surface, but there is a dangerous hill between these two towns in either direction. Principal objects of interest: Nuneaton Church, Hinckley, fine view : Market Bosworth, battlefield 1485.' On the whole, surfaces had improved, but there were still too many 'bumpy', 'cut up' or 'loose'. These little pocket books contained lamp-lighting tables, town plans and a brief gazetteer, a 'slate' for notes and a page headed 'riding summary'. They also showed railway rates for the conveyance of bicycles and tricycles—bicycles up to 400 miles 5s as luggage, 7s 6d as parcels; tricycles 10s or 20s; tandems etc fifty per cent additional per seat. (Customs duty on a 'bicycle built for two' was double the single rate—as the composer of 'Daisy Bell', cycling's most famous song, learned, at all events in the USA.)

As well as special maps and guides in plenty—Rumney alone produced three cyclists' guides to England north, England south, and to the Lake District between 1899 and 1901—there were detailed, dull, or exciting accounts of tours far afield. *From the Clyde to the Jordan, In Jutland with a Cycle, Awheel to Moscow and Back, Sketches Awheel in Iberia, A New Ride to Khiva, Across Siberia on a Bicycle*—all these appeared in the last dozen years of the century to tempt and encourage those for whom

103

Wanderings in Warwickshire were not quite enough. The Pennells, Joseph and Elizabeth of Philadelphia, biographers of Whistler, were making their illustrated pilgrimages and sentimental journeys to Italy, France and the Hebrides usually on a Humber Ordinary tandem; and Vernon Lee (Violet Paget) was taking her bicycle tours in Italy—followed by a carriage with several extra pairs of boots and elegant boot-trees.

The bicycle also figured in magazines of a different type, those containing serials of adventure like *The Strand*. An issue of 1899 has an exciting instalment, by Grant Allen, of a tale set in Rhodesia, in which the heroine escapes death from the assegais of the Matabele by 'vaulting lightly on to the seat of her bicycle'—with a baby in her left arm—'and pedalling for dear life' over the great, red sand plain amidst the black smoke from burning farms and plundered homesteads. The novelty of the 'iron horse with a woman riding it played not a little on the savages' superstitious fears', but when they started to gain she was saved in the nick of time by a compatriot horseman, who changed his mount for hers— 'her short bicycling skirt, unobtrusively divided in front and at the back, made riding astride easily possible'—while he, in spite of the low seat and short crank of a woman's machine, rode full speed up a sudden slope, steering with his left hand and firing with his right three shots from his revolver into the nearest of their naked black pursuers. Heady stuff and rough going; it does not give the make of the bicycle.

Every writer who wanted to be abreast of the time was sure to play up the bicycle for all it was worth. The up-to-date detective was featured cycling all over the country in a Norfolk suit, with pockets stuffed with automatics, hot on the trail of equally up-to-date criminals. In futurist wars it was always the cyclist who was put on for any job like kidnapping the Generalissimo Grand Duke or occupying the vital crossroads on the eve of the decisive victory. Mark Twain's *Yankee at the Court of King Arthur* puts the seal on his ultra-modernism by mounting the Knights of the Round Table, also for a decisive victory, on bicycles. ... The cult went farther than the printed page. The present writer recently came across 'Bikee, A novel and very amusing Game', issued in the period 1895-1900 by Faulkner & Company, London, in which the players put riders on 'safeties' through all kinds of unsafe manoeuvres and obstacles—something like 'Snakes and Ladders' combined with 'Halma'.

For the tourist's technical guidance and exchange of 'tips' there was also a proliferation of cycling journals and magazines. *Wheeling*, started in 1884, lasted out the Queen's reign. Its short-lived rival, *Wheel Life*, gave A. C. Harmsworth (press-magnate-to-be Lord Northcliffe) his journalistic start and A. W. Rumney an opening to contribute *Cambridge Notes*. When *Wheel Life* was incorporated with *Bicycling News* (founded 1876) Harmsworth acted as sub-editor under Lacy Hillier, who was considerably annoyed by a laudatory article on the first pneumatic tyres, which his sub-editor published. Hillier later was co-author with Viscount Bury of the Badminton Library volume on Cycling, 1887. Henry Sturmey was editor for seventeen years of *The Cyclist* (1879-1903), until in fact he had become editor of *The Autocar*, which first appeared in 1895. *The Lady Cyclist*, a monthly begun in that year, had W. W. Jacobs's sister as assistant editor—but died after twelve months. *Cycling* appeared first in January 1891 and still goes strong. Its original manager and editors were all prominent club members, and it actually paid Rumney, its touring section writer, a fixed sum on the condition that he did not contribute to any other cycling paper except the CTC's own *Gazette* (founded 1879). The doyen and acknowledged master among cyclist artists, Frank Patterson, later lent distinction to the pages both of *Cycling* and of the *CTC Gazette* with his black and white drawings of all aspects of the cycling game. There were many other cycling journals—collectors' items now such as *The Hub*—and regular cycling features in others especially in the boom years of the trade, 1896-9.

When Francis Yeats-Brown of *Bengal Lancer* fame first left England, late in 1904, 'bicycling had only recently gone out of fashion.' When he returned, in spring 1914, 'there had arrived the era of motors which often ran for hundreds of miles without a breakdown; and aeroplanes which looped the loop. We seemed to be evolving towards a splendid Golden Age.' To one who had been out of the country for a decade the change appeared dramatic and inspiriting. The real golden age of the bicycle, however, as a vehicle for private locomotion, occurred in that interval, and by 1914 the golden age of cycling club life was scarcely halfway through its course.

Page 107 : Singer de luxe

Page 108 : 'Manchester Wheelers' club member

CHAPTER SIX

CYCLING DE LUXE

'THE BICYCLE is complementary to the steam engine, doing for the horseless individual what the steam engine does for the
community. For the proletariat it is not merely a necessity but a
great luxury too.' Beerbohm was almost correct in his appreciation
of the new 'locomotomania', though not perhaps in his reasoning—
that the bicycle gratified 'the instinct common to all stupid people,
the instinct to potter with machinery'. For those fairly well-to-do
but below the carriage class, good bicycles were cheaper to buy
and run than a riding horse; for the carriage class the convenience
and readiness of the bicycle as an extra was an undoubted attraction. Such machines were not cheap—a fully equipped Rudge
(1897) was considered a bargain at ten guineas; the high-class
models likely to be favoured in country houses or professional
circles might easily cost, as Wells noted, over £20, or something
like £200 at present-day rates. For the proletariat, to whom £5 was
a large sum in 1900, the chance of a second-hand machine would
be the only way to enjoy such a luxury. If he aspired to a new
machine at all it would be one of the assembly-built models from
mass-produced parts sold locally at competitive prices.

In general bicycle-makers of the Edwardian age were no longer innovators, but perfectionists. Their products were of the same overall pattern, although differing in their detail: the quality was of the kind which gave 'British-made' a clear superiority over any other country's manufactures. The finest cycles of this period, de luxe machines produced by a few specialised makers, are also the finest cycles of any period, and survivors are eagerly sought after today by collectors.

Some of the features available before the beginning of the new reign contributed both to efficiency and comfort. Michelin's beaded-edged pneumatic tyres made the detachment of a tyre to repair a puncture much easier. Boudard's gear, by Marcel Boudard and Henry Crawley of Nottingham, brought out in 1893 and taken up by Humbers, greatly improved performance. It geared up the road wheel to such an extent that G. P. Mills, then works manager in Humber's Beeston factory and later chief designer to Raleighs, was able to break the Lands End to John o' Groats record with its aid by eight hours, taking only 3 days 5hr 49min (see plate, p54). (His record on an Ordinary set up in 1886 had been 5 days 1hr 45min.) In the same year J. G. Kitchen of Manchester patented a pneumatic brake, operated by a rubber bulb clipped to the handle-bar. Handlebars themselves had acquired various different curves, after the straight and 'cowhorn' for Ordinaries, more suitable for touring or for racing.

Tourists now could record their mileage with a trip cyclometer —such as the American 'Veeder', 1895—and ease their progress with a variable 3-speed gear, the 'Gradient', patented by E. H. Hodgkinson in 1896, a forerunner of derailleur gears. The new 'Whippet' model a year later incorporated rim brakes, free wheel and Linley's 4-speed 'Protean' gear, patented in 1894, with its expanding chain-wheel, another indirect ancestor of the derailleur. But the gear that was to capture the market came from a late entrant into cycle manufacture—the Raleigh Cycle Company.

From their first advertisements and exhibits at the Stanley Show, 1888, Raleighs had made much of devices for the variation of gear. There were other hub gears before it, such as the Jay (1883) and then the Johnston (1895), but the one which became standard was the small Sturmey-Archer 3-speed hub gear with a single epicyclic train, patented in 1902. Its designers, Henry Sturmey and James Archer, schoolmaster and engineer, took it to the head of the firm, Frank Bowden, and it was immediately put into production by Raleighs. It had a free wheel in all gears, while shortly there was to be an improved type with handlebar instead of the earlier cross-bar control.

Of the luxury machines, of best-quality materials, manufacture and finish—the high-class 'gentlemen's bicycles'—a few stand out for design and for the continued devotion of their supporters. In a class by itself for scientific design the Dursley-Pedersen, 1893, commanded much enthusiasm. It was built from the invention of a Dane, Mikael Pedersen, by Lister & Company of Dursley, Gloucestershire, with a frame on the cantilever principle, so that every tubular member took only compression stress. The tubes, in arrangement of triangles, could therefore be of very light gauge and, at the experimental stage, with a hammock saddle the machine weighed a mere 13lb. Apart from the triangulated frame, the saddle figured with especial prominence in the Dursley-Pedersen catalogue:

> composed of silk cord, suspended or swung hammock fashion, between the seat pillar and the head of the machine, attached to the seat pillar by seven spiral springs and to the head by a strap, which can be tightened or slackened as desired, this saddle adjusts itself to every movement of the body, and allows perfect freedom for those muscles which cycling brings into play. Medical men especially praise same, as it entirely prevents perineal pressure. Its network construction affords perfect ventilation, and keeps soft and comfortable, all tendencies to saddle soreness, however long the distance ridden, being overcome.

111

This saddle took some getting into, in a double sense: firstly as it seemed to tilt under one, and secondly because of the curious sway when seated; but a week's riding made one forget such things entirely and over rough roads the seat was the best of the time.

Virtually unknown until it appeared at the Stanley Show of 1897 the Dursley-Pedersen cost £25. Between 1900 and 1915 about eight thousand were manufactured by the original Dursley-Pedersen Company (see plate, p89). 'Cantilever cycles' made by their late mechanics for Stephenson & Company of Holloway in 1920 cost from £15 15s each. Rumney, who kept up to date with his mounts, had a 'military model' Dursley-Pedersen, bought in 1901, with instantly detachable front forks and a frictionless 3-speed Pedersen hub (fitted with ball-bearings throughout), giving gears of 50, 75 and 112. Its total weight, including roadster tyres and mudguards, was 29½lb. He records his tours in France, Italy, Sicily, Spain, Portugal and Algeria and to Jerusalem on this machine, regretting afterwards only that 'I had not taken it for the four days I spent at Cairo, as the roads there are excellent, the Pyramids and Heliopolis being perhaps more pleasantly reached by cycle than by any other means'. This obviously was the bicycle for the Grand Tourist!—even in Corsica carrying 50lb of baggage and cameras he found no hills, long as they were, 'too severe for an average male rider with a variable gear'. In later days he considered that he had 'never had a better machine for severe touring', supporting the maker's claim that it was both light and comfortable, and capable of standing the roughest wear and tear. Rumney eventually presented this machine to the Bartleet Collection. The Dursley-Pedersen was so durable that models have been in use for as long as fifty years. The ladies' model 'Royal', perhaps the most scientifically constructed bicycle ever produced, managed to preserve full triangulation even with an open frame, without any sacrifice of stiffness and strength.

The complete description of the Dursley-Pedersen Gentleman's

'Model Royal' with specification and prices reads as follows:

Finish	Beautifully Nickel-plated and Polished and Burnished Copper throughout: or, if preferred. enamelled in Green, Black, Claret or other Colours.
Frame	Dursley-Pedersen, built with finest quality weldless steel tubing, especially selected for plating.
Sizes	No. 1. No 1 ... No 8

Suitable for an inside leg
measure fork to ground

(fitted with 6½in cranks) of	In 27½	38
WHEELS—front and back	In 24	28
TYRES—Dunlop	In 1	1½
CRANKS—special design	6½	7½

Gear Case	Carter-Pedersen detachable oil bath (if required and if extra weight not objected to).
Gear	70in or to order.
Pedals	Extra quality Rat Trap, felt or rubber.
Freewheels and Brakes	If only one gear is required this bicycle is fitted with either a combined Free Wheel Hub and two rim brakes, or with a back pedalling coaster hub. All bicycles with variable gears are fitted with the Pedersen two hand rim brakes. Back pedalling rim brakes can be fitted in combination with variable gear (except when gear case is fitted) at an extra cost of 15s nett.
Mudguards	Detachable plated steel.
Handlebar and Saddle	Saddle—Dursley-Pedersen adjustable, extra finish.
Handles	Finest quality, white felt, cork or celluloid.
Equipment	Tool bag, spanners, pump and clips.
Prices	£16 16s—£18 18s (with 3-speed gear).
Weight	From 23lb (without free wheel and extra brake) according to size. Equipment—1¼lb; gear case 1½lb.

At their agents' request Dursley-Pedersen later put on the market ladies' and gentlemen's 'Diamond Royals' at popular prices.

113

Of the 'Sunbeam' produced by John Marston & Company, Wolverhampton, it is perhaps sufficient to record that the hand-made 'Golden Sunbeam' (1902) survived practically unaltered as long as the firm itself survived—until 1936. It had an integral oil-bath chain case, two-speed epicyclic bracket-type gear, an all-weather finish and was manufactured of the highest-grade material to very fine limits. A 1910 model 'Sunbeam' probably came as near to the acme of perfection in workmanship as it is possible for the bicycle to reach.

Lea-Francis, Beeston Humber, and Singer (see plate, p107) were other makers of de luxe bicycles in the Edwardian period. Lea and Francis specialised in the more expensive type of machine, incorporating most of the available refinements, including their own 3-speed epicyclic hub gear and a second horizontal top tube, giving a weight of 40lb. Chain case, stirrup brakes, fine leather sprung saddle, mounting step, handlegrips, bell and lamp bracket, easily detachable tyres with sturdy tread and rubber-covered pedals, were other features of an easy-running model with standards of finish which made for proud ownership—and a cost of £24 (1910).

Pride in possession of some of these machines has not entirely waned. Members of veteran cycle clubs and individual collectors in their advertisements of machines 'wanted' probably refer to the Dursley-Pedersen, the Marston 'Sunbeam' and the Lea-Francis more than to any other machines. It is still possible to see and admire on a veteran outing such models as an 1899 Chater-Lea, a 1900 Raleigh or Dursley-Pedersen, a 1910 Lea-Francis, being put through their paces among the even older Safeties and Ordinaries. Their riders go to great lengths to rehabilitate these 'gems of machines', fitting them out where defective with all the appropriate period accessories.

Raleighs—so-called from the workshop in Raleigh Street, Nottingham, where a small cycle business had been founded by three mechanics—were fortunate in the early interest taken in their firm

114

A BICYCLE DIAGRAM AND KEY.—

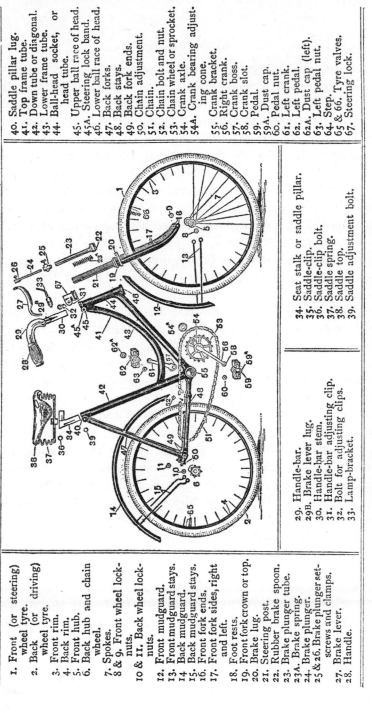

1. Front (or steering) wheel tyre.
2. Back (or driving) wheel tyre.
3. Front rim.
4. Back rim.
5. Front hub.
6. Back hub and chain wheel.
7. Spokes.
8 & 9. Front wheel lock-nuts.
10 & 11. Back wheel lock-nuts.
12. Front mudguard.
13. Front mudguard stays.
14. Back mudguard.
15. Back mudguard stays.
16. Front fork ends.
17. Front fork sides, right and left.
18. Foot rests.
19. Front fork crown or top.
20. Brake lug.
21. Steering post.
22. Rubber brake spoon.
23. Brake plunger tube.
23A. Brake spring.
24. Brake plunger.
25 & 26. Brake plunger set-screws and clamps.
27. Brake lever.
28. Handle.

29. Handle-bar.
29B. Brake lever lug.
30. Handle-bar stem.
31. Handle-bar adjusting clip.
32. Bolt for adjusting clips.
33. Lamp-bracket.

34. Seat stalk or saddle pillar.
35. Saddle-clip.
36. Saddle-clip bolt.
37. Saddle spring.
38. Saddle top.
39. Saddle adjustment bolt.

40. Saddle pillar lug.
41. Top frame tube.
42. Down tube or diagonal.
43. Lower frame tube.
44. Ball-head socket, or head tube.
45. Upper ball race of head.
45A. Steering lock band.
46. Lower ball race of head.
47. Back forks.
48. Back stays.
49. Back fork ends.
50. Chain adjustment.
51. Chain.
52. Chain bolt and nut.
53. Chain wheel or sprocket.
54. Crank axle.
54A. Crank bearing adjusting cone.
55. Crank bracket.
56. Right crank.
57. Crank boss.
58. Crank slot.
59. Pedal.
59A. Dust cap.
60. Pedal nut.
61. Left crank.
62. Left pedal.
62A. Dust cap (left).
63. Left pedal nut.
64. Step.
65 & 66. Tyre valves.
67. Steering lock.

An exploded diagram of a Safety bicycle with list of components by a customer, himself a retired businessman, who had begun to cycle for health reasons. Frank Bowden publicised his cycling 'cure', acquired an interest in the Raleigh Street works, went on to purchase the business and to develop it with great commercial acumen. From a concern producing three bicycles a week and employing twelve men, the Raleigh Cycle Company had expanded, by 1896, into the largest cycle factory in the country with a capital of £200,000, a production rate reaching 12,000 cycles a year (at the century's end), 850 workpeople and already a name for quality machines. They produced one of the best high-standard Safeties. Their factory in America, to which only 'stuff in the rough' was sent from Nottingham, was turning out 200 first-class machines per week, built to order for customers who knew that 'the best is cheapest in the end'.

Bowden, later Sir Frank, showed a flair for assessing the prospects of new devices. On the basis of his expectations for Sturmey and Archer hub gears. Raleigh formed a subsidiary company to take over their manufacture and marketing, at a price progressively reduced from £3 3s to £1. With this invaluable accessory—of which by 1913 some hundred thousand per year were being made—to their 'all-steel' bicycle, of pressed steel components and light butt-ended tubes joined by immersion brazing, the firm's fortunes were soundly established. Another fine bicycle had entered its long and useful life. And when most of the hand-made de luxe models had become too expensive to produce, their type may be said to have survived in the Raleigh 'Superbe' Tourist, which combined the complete range of accessories—including hub dynamo, fork lock and 4-speed hub gear—with both strength and lightness of construction.

IN COMPETITION

The Raleigh road racer of 1892 became famous as the machine on which the American 'crack', A. A. Zimmerman, then regarded as the fastest sprinter ever seen on the track (starting his career in 1887 he won over 1,400 races all over the world), won the British National Championships at one, five and fifty miles. The first two races were held at Headingley, Leeds, the last at Paddington Recreation Ground, London. His Raleigh A1 racer, with cut-out head lugs and brazed up seat stays, had a special system of spoking the rear wheel, a set of direct radial spokes reinforced by eight tangent spokes. It weighed 24¾lb, in contrast to the 'Star' Ordinary he used, weighing 72lb. Zimmerman was an amateur up to this time and at the first World's Championship meeting in Chicago, 1893, won the one-mile and ten-kilometre titles, 'pedalling away from the field as if some unseen force held it back'. Before he turned professional the NCU offered him a 'conditional licence'. In these days of rampant 'shamateurism' a licence might be granted to a crack rider on the condition that he rode bicycles of any other make than the one in which he was believed to have a financial interest.

Cycling, and in many respects the bicycle too, had reached a height of popularity and perfection which it was not to exceed or even reach again. 'Directly he gets on wheels he is as cocky as if he owned the universe,' noted the *Windsor Magazine* of the schoolboy of 1906: 'his manner to boys who have only their feet to take them along is always patronising, and occasionally insolent.' The attitude was no doubt in some measure imitated from the adult.

Several trends, however, in a gradual falling off became evident. The brief society 'boom' was already over: even footlights favourites, like Mabel Love, posed less often with their sleek ladies' machines. Some of the old pioneering firms had been ruined in the sudden inflation. Between 1900 and 1905 more than three-fifths of the American manufacturers went out of business. A public which had turned out in its thousands on the race tracks at Crystal Palace and elsewhere, to witness such spectacles as the pacing of crack riders by teams of highly trained professionals on 'quadruplets' and 'quintets' sponsored by Dunlops and others, began to fade away. The reason is not clear : there was dissatisfaction both with the 'fixing of races' and with 'shamateurism' in a period of intense rivalry among the cycle-makers, and even more between the two leading tyre manufacturers, so that track stars could command not only 'appearance money' and payment for successes but cash in lieu of the advertised prizes as well. At one time, indeed, the 'un-licensed brigade', consisting of riders who could not obtain amateur licences and would not apply for the professional ticket, was in quality the strongest section of the racing community. Or, again, cycling's loss may have been part of the change of interest to some other craze. Indoor skating, for instance, entered upon a fresh wave of popularity about 1908-9, leading to 'rinkomania'. In the latter year an affair of internal politics in the CTC deteriorated from dissension to open quarrel, which came close to destroying the club. Inevitably it must have deterred many from entering the cycling world. CTC membership dropped to 40,000 in a single decade, and at the end of the war only 8,500 cyclists remained in the fold. Within another decade, however, numbers were to rise again to 25,000.

And while the abandonment of massed-start road races in the nineties, in favour of 'time trials', had cut Britain off from con tinental-type racing, a new, noisier occupant of the road was now receiving maximum attention. The Hon C. S. Rolls was not alone in his change of allegiance. Even Rumney was tempted—for an instant—away from cycling: 'I began [in autumn 1909] a flir-tation with motoring, buying an old "quad" : but soon abandoned it as being too troublesome as well as not giving one the right feeling of freedom on the road.'

The 'quad' was one example of a race which, owing much of its early development to the bicycle and its designers and engineers, as soon as it came to the forefront began to usurp and endanger the cyclist's place on the roads. 'Tuff-tuff', the innocent sound of a 'horseless carriage' tricycle doing 15 mph in 1896 on some Herefordshire road—and subsequently the name given to a French veteran car club—was soon to reverberate with greatly multiplied and magnified resonance all over the country. As cars and motorcycles became available in increasing numbers—until in the early 1920s a small car could be bought for £100—so cycle production, especially of the luxury model, began to decline.

The bicycle industry had itself provided the means and facilities for its rival's rapid growth. Most of the fundamental parts of cars related back to inventions or their developments made for bicycles: weldless steel tubing, wire-spoked wheels, pneumatic tyres, Bown's adjustable ball-bearings (patented 1877), the freewheel clutch, the differential gear, Ackermann steering (invented for tandem tricycles), the William Starley 'live' axle (also for tricycles), variable speed gears, all contributed to the swift, practical evolution of the automobile, and were first employed by the cycle trade. Not only motoring mechanics but pioneer firms involved in car manufacture —in Britain Hillman and Humber, Rover and Singer, not to mention Morris in his Cowley workshop, in the USA Pierce, Lozier, Pope, and, also, the flying Wright Bros—owed much to experience with the bicycle. J. K. Starley himself had begun to build the first 'Rover'—the prototype of an electrically-powered tri-car—in his Coventry works in 1888, even while the Rover bicycle was still catching on with the public. And, ironically, the roads which cars were increasingly to monopolise had been improved and signposted —the 'Good Roads' movement of the eighties—first by the official cycling organisations. In 1898 a well-known cyclist, Fitzwater Wray, found the Great North Road between Grantham and Stamford grass-grown and stony, with only two wheel tracks to ride upon. After the introduction in 1903 of 'Westrumite' dust-laying spray, county road surveyors using 'tarmac' (cubes of granite or other hard stone immersed in tar) showed that they could make smooth and rutless roads for motor vehicles.

The anomalies of the situation still occur. The CTC continues its road campaign. 'Consider the cyclist: don't place him in unnecessary danger from bad surfaces, neglected edges, gulley gratings and metal studs.' Even in the 1960s it could point out closely placed studs remaining in roads, despite Ministry of Transport recommendations, sides of roads almost unusable by cyclists, and conditions which drivers of other vehicles would not tolerate near the centre line of the carriageway—while they regarded as obstructive any cyclist who kept well away from the kerb to avoid these hazards.

While the bicycle's status peak was passing, however, club life and track performance suffered no eclipse. W. J. Bailey of the Polytechnic CC, V. L. Johnson of Rover Racing CC and L. Meredith, Paddington CC, were heaped with honours between 1902 and 1914 wherever championships were held, and these trackmen were regarded as among the world's best. In the nineties there had been a four-year period of British domination of the 100km motor-paced event at Cologne, the British world champions being Michael in 1895, Chase in 1896, Stocks in 1897 and Palmer in 1898. Of the twenty-one amateur champions of the 100km paced events held between 1893 and 1914 nine were British, and Leon Meredith's name occurred among them no fewer than seven times. From 1896 to 1913 the amateur sprint, however, proved to be England's real forte. Reynolds won the world title in 1896, Summersgill in 1899, Reed in 1903, Benyon in 1905, V. L. Johnson in 1908 and W. J. Bailey 1909-11, and then again in 1913. Donald McDougal, USA, was the 1912 winner. (After the war there was to be an interval of twenty-five years between H. T. Johnson's winning of this event in 1922, and the first of Reg Harris's victories as an amateur champion.) Bailey became a well-known figure at the Newark velodrome, New Jersey—a wooden, saucer-shaped track with arc lamps for evenings race meetings—and on the circuit of tracks at Boston,

Providence and Philadelphia, as a contract rider in the post-war heyday of American cycle racing.

In August 1908 A. E. Mills beat the world record for one hour paced on the Munich track, by covering 61miles 972yd on a BSA racing bicycle, and was thus the first man to ride at a speed of a mile a minute for sixty minutes, from a standing start.

On the road, where unpaced records had been established from 1898 and the first world championship held in 1921, the only British world success was by Dave Marsh in 1922, after which there was to be an unsuccessful interval extending nearly forty years. Marsh won the amateur *Championnat du Monde* gold medal on the famous Anfield '100' course over the hills and rough roads of north Shropshire, beating the previous year's winner at Copenhagen, Skold of Sweden, by more than a minute with a time of 5hr 7min 27sec on the time trial system. It seemed a battle between a pocket Hercules and a Scandinavian 'giant of the road'— but English riders took second and third places also.

The history of the Anfield club reveals that the period 1899-1914 was one of great achievement in the pursuit of unpaced records recognised by the Northern Roads Records Association, both on single bicycles, tandems and tricycles. Of the fifty-two NRRA records made in those years, thirty were by Anfielders and another ten RRA unpaced records were broken by members—remarkable testimony to club spirit and strength.

Another feature of the period was the formation of the Association of Cycle Campers in 1901, with a first meeting at Oxford. The chief founder member, T. H. Holding, designed and made light tents with a maximum weight of two pounds. After a merger with the Camping Club in 1909 the association became the Amateur Camping Club, which in turn subsequently developed into the Camping Club of Great Britain and Ireland, after a period just before World War II when it was known as the Association of Cycle and Light-Weight Campers. The idea surely would have appealed to those

121

early tourists who had carried their all in a Sturmey 'take-about' or a *multum in parvo* en route for Fort William!

General guide books to picturesque districts now as a rule gave advice to two classes: the pedestrian, and the cyclist or motorist. Ward Lock's *Guide to the English Lake District* (19th edn, 1922), for example, has notes such as these:

> Cycling in Lakeland is enjoyable, if arduous. The triangles and other signs for motor traffic erected by the County Council serve equally well for the cyclist and should be carefully regarded, especially on inclines and long mountain passes. During the past twenty years there has been considerable improvement both on main roads and by-ways. Surfaces throughout are well made, and dangerous corners have been almost eliminated in the central area. Cyclists should note that some of the by-roads are still crossed by gates; a sharp look-out should be kept for them. Cycling in the outlying districts is less severe, but the ups and downs are numerous and often abrupt and less official attention has been paid to improvements.

In the course of particularising certain roads and risks, such as Dunmail Raise (where the descent from the north requires care), Red Bank (unquestionably very dangerous for cyclists), and Ferry Hill (preferably *not* to be descended) the writer of the guide makes clear that some of the perils formerly attendant on the cyclist only are now lying in wait for the motorist, and also that the car itself brings new perils to the cyclist.

> The ascent from or descent to Ambleside [of the Kirkstone Pass] is out of the question. The only reasonable course for cycle or motor is by way of Troutbeck. It is all uphill till the summit of the Pass is reached: thence to Brothers' Water it is dangerously steep downhill. The surface is good throughout, but the collar-work is fatiguing and the descent dangerous. Motorists are warned that should the car run away with them (as it may), not everyone can have the luck to charge a stone wall, knock it down, have the car turn over on him, and

then walk healthily on to the hotel. This has actually occurred on this route, but it is unwise to expect a recurrence of miracles . . .

Between Keswick and Seatoller there are numerous ups and downs, some of them quite sharp. The cyclist has always to be vigilant, for, despite improvements, the lane is still narrow, and hedged by tall stone walls which mask the approach of the modern low motor car. From Seatoller it is almost all push to Honister House. Here the cyclist must on no account mount, but must walk down the rough pass till the comparatively level ground at the foot of Honister Crag is reached. This route is not for motorists.

Honours about even, then. But on the motorist's side, as harbinger of the touring future, there was already a pioneer of direct motor service, between Penrith and Patterdale, in the shape of a solid-tyred, open-sided omnibus.

Obviously de luxe machines, track racing and club fixtures were not the be-all and end-all of bicycling in the first two decades of the twentieth century. The average man and woman rider, who took to the bicycle for a combination of utility and pleasure in such numbers that Raleighs alone were turning out fifty thousand machines each year from their Nottingham factory by the beginning of World War I, provided the staple element in both cycle traffic and trade. As the comparatively well-off New Woman of Wells's romance had first tasted freedom and adventure on her £20 machine, so in the early short stories of D. H. Lawrence one finds frequent mention of the bicycle and the opportunities it affords as a means of escape from stuffy vicarage life, easing contact with the outside world for a pair of independent young women living together, or as ready-and-waiting conveyance for soldiers in barracks seeking weekend dalliance. It is a symbol still of freedom in this middle- and lower-middle-class world. Among the intelligentsia, G. B. Shaw and the Bloomsbury group it is almost a fetish.

New companies came into being alongside the old, such as Rudge, Triumph, Swift, New Hudson: large-scale producers who made complete bicycles of sound design, but with economy of production, to market throughout the country, and local firms which assembled machines from mass-produced parts, bought from manufacturers such as BSA, Chater-Lea, Abingdon-Ecco, to sell competitively in their own districts. Wartime naturally led to a big reduction in output, but until the mid-twenties such decline was largely limited to the luxury trade, although some of the smaller specialist firms, who were finding competition too hot, had gone out of business before 1914. This kind of firm, which would employ craftsmen each able to make every component of a bicycle himself —producing parts individually to match, not to gauge, cutting, mitring and brazing their tubes, drilling and tapping from stampings hub cones and then turning them on a lathe with the spindle, doing their own plating, enamelling and lining—perhaps depended on two or three frame-builders, three or four fitters, a wheel-builder, say a score or so of workmen altogether: and depended also a good deal on local patronage. *Its* days clearly were numbered.

Page 125 : Time trialist—Holland of 'Manchester Wheelers'

Page 126 : Professional sprint champion Reg Harris beats Kain
(Austria), 25 August 1951

CHAPTER SEVEN

ON CIVIL AND MILITARY OCCASIONS

FROM THE beginning the bicycle, to a limited extent, entered the public service. The improved Draisienne led the way as a French rural postman's machine in 1830, its use being brought to an end by a particularly bad winter season. The British Post Office tried out its successor, the velocipede, with a few bought or hired machines; then, in 1880, established two tricycle posts in the cycle centre, Coventry. Their riders received a weekly allowance to cover purchase and maintenance costs. It was at least a start.

Two years later a special machine suitable for Post Office purposes was produced by Gibbons. It was a pentacycle, often described as the 'centre-cycle', and had a large wheel in the centre, two small ones at each end with a bracket above each pair to support a basket. From its appearance it was usually called, not as its maker intended, 'The Ideal', but the 'Hen and Chickens'. The design provided that, in motion, the small wheels could be raised leaving in effect a monocycle machine. (Though sometimes the reverse happened: the four small wheels would jam, raising the

127

central one so that the rider was left pedalling in space.) Its production was timely: the introduction of parcel post in 1883 considerably increased the loads which rural postmen had to carry and, as a photograph shows, a postman loaded with two body satchels, two side panniers and two large baskets could cope with a good deal. The 'Hen and Chickens' had its first trial in the Horsham district: another early photograph shows five postmen similarly mounted setting out from the sheds. But its local success was not sufficient to recommend it generally, in view of its excessive size and weight, and this experiment also came to an end.

For another dozen years mail delivered by cycle was a comparative rarity: during that time there were only sixty-seven such postal services, Bayliss, Thomas & Company having obtained the first contract for the supply of carrier tricycles. Delivery of telegrams, however, either by tricycle or bicycle, soon gained ground. The riders provided their own machines and were entitled to a weekly allowance for upkeep. Eventually, in 1896, the Post Office purchased a hundred cycles and, as telegrams and postal traffic continued to increase, followed this up during another eight years with further orders of machines to an official specification. Extended use of bicycles was a natural concomitant of the extension, at the time of Queen Victoria's Diamond Jubilee in 1897, of the free delivery of telegrams from a radius of one mile to three miles, and coincided also with the general cycling boom.

From 1904 to 1929 normal trade-pattern machines were again purchased for the Post Office cycle service and maintenance parts for each make kept in stock. With the very large increase in the total of the 'fleet' and the area of its operation over those twenty-five years, however, local stock maintenance of spares for a variety of machines became too complex and costly. Manufacturers were by then already standardising constituent parts and so the Post Office decided to re-equip, by stages, with a machine selected for hard service. It was made up of standard components, with frames and forks that could be produced by any of the leading manufacturers with their existing equipment: a Post Office bicycle, in fact, in substance as well as in colour and in name, was economically constructed. The trade-pattern machines, after 1928, were accordingly phased out.

Several particular requirements for public service had to be kept in view. High-quality material and workmanship was essential. Grade 'A' quality steel tubing, bearings made with steel to the standard demanded in aircraft material, components subject to inspector's analysis or tests for hardness—these were some of the requirements. A suitable single gear, usually 65in, dependable headlamp, water-proof saddle, were other desiderata. Parts for repairs, accessories etc—some three hundred all told—were obtained direct from the original manufacturers, examined, and then stored centrally for distribution as required. It was a more economical way of maintaining a large fleet which, within five years from this change in supply, provided a service to over five hundred towns and to many more than that number of villages throughout Great Britain and Northern Ireland.

From the simple wooden construction of the hobbyhorse and velocipede to the solid wrought-iron frame of the boneshaker, then to hollow frames and forks in the Ordinary and solid-drawn mild steel tubes with brazed wrought-iron lugs and brackets in the Safeties, the constructive process had been towards thinner tubes and lighter steel stampings, with liquid brazing methods of Raleigh's innovation and BSA's drop-forging method of manufacturing cycle parts. The pattern of progress had thus been towards strength with lightness, simplification of assembly, and standardisation: mass-production methods by large concerns added the fourth factor, economy. The first factor was reinforced in the mid-thirties by the availability of Accles & Pollocks chrome-molybdenum cycle frame parts, stronger, lighter, fatigue-resisting and not weakened by brazing; and by Reynold's 531 butted steel tubes of manganese molybdenum steel, which provided extra metal where stress was greatest while permitting thinner tubes, The latter company also supplied hiduminium handlebars and stem, an aluminium alloy with a weight only one-third that of steel. New Hudson, at about the same time, evolved a frame built of pressed steel members bolted together instead of brazed, that was light, strong, rigid and easy both to assemble and to repair.

Such developments were taken into consideration by the Post Office as their new fleet of bicycles continued to grow and improvements in design or material of components were utilised where suitable, trials being regularly conducted with any promising alternative. To maintain his machine in good condition was the rider's responsibility and an allowance was paid. Cleaning materials, tyre repair outfits, a booklet with name-chart of all parts, and instructions for minor adjustments, were issued to him. Regular inspection of machines, especially of the front forks, blades and stem, on which a weight load of up to 50lb might be carried, helped to insure against injury to rider or damage to bicycle. The forks, in view both of the extra weight and the rough roads and farm tracks over which deliveries were made, had special strength : steel liners were brazed to the blades and there was a circular steel liner in the stem, but not brazed, so as to serve as an independent support in event of stem fracture. All such machines and parts had their supplier's guarantee for twelve months' service without failure. Examination both by stores inspectors and contractors was not only a considerable help in maintaining quality, but sometimes in improving design after seeing the results of such stringent road testing.

The postman was not the only public servant to use the bicycle, in line of duty, at a comparatively early stage. In the nineties it was believed that there was a great future, in outlying districts and country towns, for the fireman's cycle. A contemporary photograph, taken in the neighbourhood of Brighton at that period, shows a quadricycle 'fire engine', two tandems joined together, with four brass-helmeted riders mounted two abreast. The pumps are being worked by the pedals, with the back wheels thrown off the ground, and four or five firemen are standing by to secure the connection with the hydrant, direct the hose and keep back the inevitable group of spectators.

A policeman's cycle—apart from that in general use on rural beats until recently in Britain—also put in an appearance. The Davis Sewing Machine Company of Dayton, Ohio, manufactured it in 1897/8 for use by various police departments in several American cities. Known as the 'Police Patrol Tricycle', the machine provided front and rear seats for the policemen and a seat in the middle for a prisoner, who had his back to the foremost rider and hands and feet securely strapped. As a means of conveying offenders to the lock-up it may have supplied a much-needed want, but, with its marked resemblance to a mechanical wheelbarrow, it remained, as the company claimed, unique. The bicycle was also pressed into detective service for race-course week in the midnineties. On Epsom Downs at the Derby Day carnival there were quite a number of detectives awheel, on the *qui-vive* for the 'welsher', and from the number of delinquents appearing next day before the magistrates the cycling detective appeared to have been a very successful experiment.

Another evanescent application of cycling, on a machine probably the longest ever built, was that practised at the Royal Normal College for the Blind, Norwood. This 'bicycle', with its twelve pairs of wheels and heavy Dunlop tyres, was designed to carry twelve riders 'for exhilarating spins in the college grounds'. It was necessary, of course, for one of the crew to have his sight: number 2 on the machine was the one responsible for steering. He can have had no easy task negotiating corners on the gravel paths, even at the pace likely on this unparalleled multi-cycle. The American Orient Cycle Company made, in 1896, for use unspecified, a bicycle built for ten.

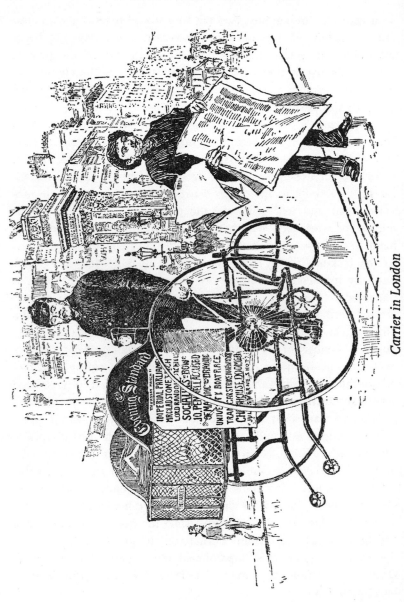

Carrier in London

On unofficial occasions, in the heyday of its fame, the bicycle ran the gamut of use and misuse as a utility, a novelty, a 'gimmick' and a hybrid. Carrier tricycles, designed by Alldays & Onions on Safety bicycle lines, served the needs of delivery men, newspaper vendors, and errand boys with little alteration in design from the nineties for well over a generation. During the boom years manufacturers, both of cycles and of other commodities, sought to bring their goods to public notice by a variety of startling innovations and oddities. A two-wheel Safety, built for show purposes by the makers of Cleveland bicycles, USA, had 15ft diameter wheels, 18in single-tube tyres, 6in tubing, ¾in thick spokes, and a gear of 360in. It could not be ridden; but the tricycle manufactured for Boston Rubber Company to advertise 'Vim' tyres *could*. When it was exhibited in a London cycle store dismantling was necessary before it could be set in position. This monster toured to Brighton with eight riders. It had 11ft side wheels, a 7ft steering wheel, 15in and 18in tyres, and ½in steel spokes. It was geared to 54in and, although it weighed nearly a ton, its finely made bearings allowed it to be pushed on level ground by one man. At the other end of the scale, in Britain, a diminutive machine, called the 'Tit-Bits' cycle, made an appearance at Bradford cycle show. This model had 10in wheels, a 3in crank, gear 22in, and could be ridden under an ordinary dining-room table by its possessor, the seventeen-month-old son of the local Cycle and Motor Company's manager.

A bicycle designed to run on railway track—to reach the scene of an accident or some distant signal box—was produced in America. It had a third, small wheel set on a stayed extension rod at the appropriate interval alongside, flat-surfaced wheels without tyres, and could travel easily at 20mph. A bicycle to sail on dry land was also fitted out. This 'bicycle yacht' had a 10ft mast, secured to the frame behind the handlebars, and a sail controlled by the rider by means of a cord passing along the boom to the handlebars, without interfering with his steering. Its appeal to 'wheelmen who are fond of excitement with just a dash of danger' appears to have been limited. In this country Gaunt's 'cycloplane'— which Rumney tried out on a tandem—had a mast and 5ft 'penthouse' but frightened every horse it met although it 'was not so absurd as expected'. The Crypto Cycle Company exhibited at the Stanley Show of 1893 a 'tandem boat' capable of a speed of 7¾mph for use either by lady and gentleman or by two gentlemen. Finally, a Brooklyn, New York, inventor produced the bicycle skate. Machines suffered still more gimmickry in this most bicycle-conscious era. One, made in Omaha to advertise a Stove Repair Works, had all its component parts made out of those of an ordinary stove. In Semaphore, South Australia, an ironmonger exhibited a machine and rider made entirely from articles on sale in his store, such as grindstones, gas-tongs, hammers, and augers. Tiffany & Company, the celebrated jewellers, went one better. A lady's Ordinary diamond dropped-frame bicycle was modelled and exhibited by them in their New York showroom, of which every part was of precious or semi-precious material: silver frame with rococo ornamentation, ivory and jade handles, silver brakes, bell and cyclometer, solid silver lamp with ruby and emerald cut-crystal sidelights, nickel-plated mudguard strung with silk. It appeared only for one day before being purchased by a titled Englishman. Other machines, anticipating the fashion of the gold-plated Daimler of one of our more individualistic millionaires, were made of gold, silver, ivory parts or ornament, and diamond or amethyst mountings to a size which could be ridden. A tandem in this style, of American manufacture and costing £2,000, appeared—the most expensive machine on record—but whether such bicycles were ever seen on a road is another question.

WAR SERVICE

In one field, however, the machine was treated according to regu-

lations and with respect. On the continent alert military interest
was taken in the bicycle at quite an early stage, so that by the
eighties both Ordinary bicycles and tricycles were in use for accel-
erating troop movements. The Italian army used cyclists for carrying messages in manœuvres as early as 1875. Ten years or so later
the French used military cyclists as despatch riders. Before long
the French and the Austrian armies were carrying out trials with
a folding cycle, 28lb in weight, which could be borne on an
infantryman's back and assembled within thirty seconds.

It was believed that such 'mechanised infantry' would provide
an effective fighting unit and so solve many of the problems of war.

A portable bicycle for the military cyclist

135

For reconnaissance, despatch bearing, guerilla action, medical and ambulance duties, patrols and the tasks of sappers, the cyclist's speed, silence and secrecy would be invaluable. And with its rifles on the cross-bar a unit could be concealed by the smallest amount of cover, come almost instantly into action and, if required, cover up to fifty miles a day. Such units would be as fast again as cavalry, almost self-maintained and practically inconspicuous when moving by night, even with large formations.

In England a suggestion was made in the press, in June 1882, by the Hon R. G. Molyneux, to form a volunteer *corps d'élite* mounted on bicycles; but the Ordinary was felt to be unsuitable and nothing came of it. The first recorded employment of cyclists for actual military purposes came in 1885. At the Easter manœuvres the adjutant of the Brighton Rifles (Volunteers) faced an 'enemy' with mounted troops. Major Bloomfield, the adjutant, borrowed revolvers from the coastguards and issued them to members of his unit whom he then 'mounted'—on Ordinaries.

When the Safety came into prominence Colonel A. T. Savile, Professor of Tactics at the Royal Staff College, Camberley, and himself a keen cyclist, gave his enthusiastic support to a military cyclist movement. He was the first to muster a parade, however motley, of military cyclists—on a Canterbury Cricket ground, in 1887. In October the same year experiments were conducted at Aldershot, where riding at logs etc—a sort of obtacle course for cyclists—took place. In the USA experiments were made also in 1887 at the North-Western Military Academy, Wisconsin with a team of cadets who scaled walls while carrying bicycles equipped with clips for rifles and other warlike gear.

Major Edge of the Royal Marines Light Infantry, Walmer, sought and was granted permission, but no official support, for forming a corps of volunteer military cyclists. It was considered that the bicycle could prove a serviceable 'horse' for the use of the Marines, as it could be stowed aboard ship where it would take less room and would need neither care nor food before engaging in active service. The War Office appointed a committee, with Colonel Savile as chairman, and G. Lacy Hillier and Henry Sturmey among its members, which sat in the Levée room at Horse Guards and then inspected the machines in St Stephen's Hall of the Royal Aquarium. The committee's report had more than the usual share of success.

In 1888 came the formation of the 26th Middlesex (Cyclist) Volunteer Rifle Corps—the first army unit consisting purely of cyclists—with Colonel Savile as commanding officer. The cyclists were divided into troops by their machines: Ordinaries, Safeties, Tricycles, etc. The establishment, at first 121 of all ranks, was soon increased to 361. There were further experiments, including one with a 'Flying Sapper'—a dozen men on a machine not unlike that used at the Royal Normal College for the Blind, towing a larger trailer of engineering tools—but, like the first cycle machine-gun (1891) ridden by two men, it broke down. Lord Wolseley's view, that the day was coming when large bodies of cyclists would become integral parts of every army in the field, was echoed by the Belgian War Department which made thorough preparations for utilising bicycles to mobilise troops. (Belgium had some admirable roads and a generally level terrain.) The possibility of using the bicycle for laying and retrieving temporary telegraph and telephone wires was tested, in 1896, in the Signal Corps of the United States Army.

Already, therefore, before the South African War underlined the potential, the bicycle had a part in military thinking and activities. During the last decade of the old and the first of the new century many Volunteer Rifle Corps followed the example of the 26th Middlesex, forming their own cycling sections of varying strengths. A regulation passed in 1901 allowed Rifle Volunteer Corps with establishments of over 600 to have cyclist companies, whose minimum establishment would be seventy-five. The Cyclist Manœuvres of 1906 saw fifty cyclist companies represented, but realising the inadequacy of company organisation for combined work the authorities inclined towards battalions. The following year Colonel Gilbertson Smith, then commanding the 26th, was authorised to bring his command strength up to 500. When Territorial Forces were formed in 1908 an additional nine cyclist battalions were formed, and by the outbreak of war the number of these battalions reached fourteen.

A War Office training and drill manual, 1907, listed special signals and parade ground commands for the cycle units, with details of inspection procedure. At one point, instructions were issued to provide the same gear ratio in army cycles—so that they could travel at the same speed or 'keep in step'. Tactical devices such as the hollow square ('zariba'), surrounded by a fence of bicycles (instead of the original Sudanese thorn-bush enclosure) as defence against cavalry, were put into action. A machine-gun tricycle of Rudge-Whitworth manufacture had trials. It mounted two guns on its two-seater tandem frame, with supports coming on to the ground when it was in action, firing from the rear. The Pope Manufacturing Company developed a bicycle mounting a Colt automatic machine gun for the United States Army. There was also a military tandem bicycle complete with rifle supports, revolver holster and pouches, and a 'Duplex' with rapid firing gun aimed over the handlebars. In 1899 there were further demonstrations of a quadricycle armed with a Maxim gun and a protective shield and ammunition carrier. The African War saw the use of a Safety bicycle with a folding frame to facilitate its transport, produced by BSA.

Cyclists were keen to prove their ability and readiness before World War I. They played an impressive part in the Royal Tournament of 1909, and shared also the surprise mobilisations, units mustering up to 90 per cent of their strength at HQ and travelling by night to locations some seventy miles away within 9½ hours. Many champion cyclists were pulled in by the recruiting posters of

1912. Soldiers in gaiters, stockings, mess jacket and forage cap could be seen, 'taking the ring', 'tent pegging', 'cutting the lemon', or 'cleaving the head' with sabres, mounted on Safeties. On the roads leading from barracks, platoons of cyclists in their tight dark uniforms and leather cross-straps stirred up the summer dust as they fanned out across their width, apparently regardless of other users.

In a short story written just before the war, *The Land Ironclads*, H. G. Wells pitted 'seasoned regulars', cavalry and infantry with artillery support, against 'civilised amateurs', cyclist infantry and cavalry attacking with embryonic 'monster' tanks. In a graphic and to some extent prophetic encounter the invader 'came across the frontier on the very dawn of war in half-a-dozen parallel columns behind a cloud of cyclists and cavalry'. The defender horsemen tried to 'charge cyclists in open order, with land ironclads outflanking them on either side.... Cyclists could retreat over open turf before horsemen with a sufficient margin of speed to allow of frequent dismounts and such terribly effective sharp shooting.' The conclusion was predictable: 'the multitude of townsmen soldiers on bicycles or afoot swept up the opposition like a great net in the rear of the ironclads.'

When first war broke out the territorials were unable to take their cycles across the Channel, most being required for infantry, while yeomanry cyclists became coast guards. The 25th Cyclist Battalion (motto, *'Tenax et Audax'*) went to India and had its badge carved among others on the rock-face on the north-west frontier. During the early stages of war, however, cyclist companies were attached to British divisions in France—one promptly made a surprise attack on a force of two hundred Germans and effected their surrender—and shortly the various units were formed into battalions of the Army Cyclist Corps. The folding BSA bicycle continued in production, for their use, substantially unaltered.

World War I postcards in the present writer's collection show contingents of helmeted French cyclists with haversacks on handlebars, capes strapped to rear stays and rifles on their backs proceeding past an Hôtel de Ville towards the front, behind a staff car. (Fabrique Nationale d'Armes de Guerre, Liège, was the French equivalent to BSA: they had also the folding or adjustable Gerard bicycle.) Belgian cyclists also *prêts à avancer* are depicted waiting at a roadside with their rifles and cycles stacked in pairs, capes and water bottles in use. During the campaign in France and Flanders cyclist companies were rushed up to bolster critical sections of the line on many occasions. A battalion operating with 1st King Edward's Horse in one action lost half its members and came out under a lieutenant's command. Cycle orderlies grew used to making improvised repairs under enemy shell fire. Troops struggled to push their machines through the ruined villages in torrents of rain and seas of mud during the bitter year 1917. When Gallipoli was evacuated one of the heart-breaking sights, witnessed by a colonel fresh from Mudros, was a case of forty new bicycles left in the open, their lamps stolen, 'fast congealing into a solid mass of rust, for which no one was responsible'. Although cyclist units did not achieve tactical breakthrough nor fulfil some of the expectations of the early military enthusiasts, they played a most useful part and soon developed an esprit and tradition appropriate to regiments of the line.

After the Armistice cyclist units were disbanded; but the 1st/25th (duplicated with the war's outbreak) continued to serve—in the Third Afghan War—without its cycles, being seconded to motor transport and infantry. Their story, 'The London Cyclists' Battalion', has been told in full (Foster Groom: 1932). Their badges, incorporating bicycle wheels, along with those of other cyclist battalions (such as the Hampshire wheel surmounted by a crown, rose in the centre, in red and blue enamel), their special forage cap and mess jackets, are all now eagerly sought by both cycling and war relic collectors.

On Civil and Military Occasions

One set of wartime regulations for cyclists, which affected non-military riders no less, was that enacted under DORA (Defence of the Realm Act) for the lighting of bicycles at night. Front and rear lamps were the subject of control, and of safeguards not always clarified by the verbiage of official announcements. It was forbidden, for example, for an acetylene lamp 'to consume more than 14 litres (½ cubic foot) of gas per hour'—but how could spot check testing enforce it? The lens must be covered with 'one thickness of ordinary white tissue paper', but if the gum used to affix it increased its opacity still further then there might be other grounds for complaint. The bulb of an electric lamp, if carried, must not exceed 12w and must also be covered by one thickness of white tissue paper. Were an oil lamp being used—such as an old Holophote 'King of the Road'—limitations were imposed on the width of the wick. Not more than two lights were permitted in front—in case their combined dim beams should attract the attention of Zeppelin commanders—and a third on the 'rear of the bicycle', but whether that meant back axle or back mudguard was not clear. When DORA expired, at the end of the war, the hope that rear lights on cycles at night would come to an end too was to prove vain.

Memories of events leading up to World War II, of its major actions and sequels, seem to be criss-crossed with the photographic images of cyclists: of Finnish soldiers riding, separated by equal space, rifles slung over their shoulders, along forest roads, or drawn into cover in snow-blanketed woods at the approach of enemy aircraft, or going into action with four anti-tank mines strapped to their cycle frames; of British paratroops in training and their folding bicycles—lighter than previous types, but still of the same general design as used in war since 1900, with hinges incorporated with the two main frame tubes; of Japanese troops, in the invasion of Malaya, trekking through jungle thought to be impenetrable, and holding fire crackers, on bicycles; of Parisian midinettes, conducting their own campaign against occupation by deliberately riding past

141

German troops with their skirts billowing high in tantalising provocation; of Canadians wading ashore on D-day from landing craft, carrying their bicycles through waist-deep water; of British units moving up to the crucial attack at Caen either on foot or bicycle; of German cyclist battalions supported by assault guns being hastily brought up to reinforce defences; of the German cyclist patrols guarding Allied prisoners on some long weary march to the 'cage'.

In World War II, where 'the bulk of the Wehrmacht was still dependent upon horse-drawn artillery and transport—in infantry divisions two-thirds of the vehicles and guns were drawn by horse' (*The Struggle for Europe*, by Chester Wilmot)—the cyclist might still often find himself the fastest mover in the field. On the civilian front the bicycle was called into increasing use by workers in war plants, both in Great Britain and the USA, where shortage of automobiles and rationing of tyres and gasoline helped to reintroduce a cycling habit that was remembered with favour when war ended, especially for short-distance journeys.

After one war, another. . . . The image of the cyclist scarcely attracted attention when men of the Royal Horse Guards, for instance, set off on patrol against EOKA forces in Crete (1958), only because he was a completely familiar military figure—instead of one of the motley crowd, composed of retired officers in uniform, some armed with rifle, bayonet, sword, binoculars, who had formed the first military cyclist's parade seventy-one years before. Later, in Vietnam the United States Army experienced, again, the tactics of guerilla warfare backed by 'invisible' bicycle transport, to their cost—as the French had done at Dien Bien Phu, in 1954, where thousands of Viet Minh porters and thousands of bicycles (Peugeots!) had each brought up through the jungle as much as 500lb of rice and ammunition.

At the time of writing it is announced that a team of one officer and nine soldiers of the Royal Regiment of Fusiliers will not return

Page 143 : Tourists in the mid-sixties—the girl has a 'Viking'

Page 144 : Norman Shiel, Amateur Pursuit Champion
of the World in the fifties

to England by air with the rest of their battalion when their tour of duty in Berlin ends. Instead, they have elected to cover a circuitous route of 1,528 miles on bicycles, through West Germany, Luxembourg, France, Belgium and Holland, riding about seventy-three miles a day. And aboard a newly-built supertanker officers use bicycles and the captain a tricycle (for stability) to travel quickly the length of their 370yd long ship. . . . Now, again, collectors and hoarders are acquiring and offering the 'last war' relics: 'BSA folding paratroop bike, sound but shabby—needs respraying and new tyres—derailleur gear with double chain wheel' (club advertisement, 1970).

J

CHAPTER EIGHT

THE COMPLETE CYCLIST

'TO SOME of us cycling almost becomes a way of life. It is the sharing of common experiences and consequent sharing of memories that binds together men and women of all temperaments and from all walks of life.' This writer of a letter in a cycling club gazette goes on to ask: 'What is it that makes two men, both lowly placed in a race, keep going and give everything to be 30th instead of 31st? What is it that takes them back next week, still without a chance of winning, but to suffer all over again? For most of us it is a personal battle that we are winning, a battle of our minds over our bodies. Our achievements are not measured in the official record books'.

Cycling affords a range of opportunities, probably wider than those in any physical activity except sailing, at every stage from junior to veteran, from 'tuggo' (uninitiated) and 'scrubber', 'jogger' and 'medium marker' to accomplished rider, on solitary, social and family occasions, and to any section of the community. The potterer, the pace-maker, the organiser, the 'original', the home tourist, the 'outback' camper, all have individual scope, yet common interest that will bring them closer over the years.

For the young, entry into the cycling world has already many doors, whilst they are still at a comparatively early stage in school. Those who travel to and from school by bicycle will be familiar with cycling proficiency tests conducted in co-operation with the local police, with periodical inspections of their machine's road-worthiness, and with various aspects of accident prevention and road regulations. (The National Cycling Proficiency scheme grew out of the Cycling Proficiency Test, first introduced by the Royal Society for the Prevention of Accidents, and was still administered by the latter society when sponsored by the Ministry of Transport in the 1950s—a time when motor cars were pouring out of the factories and on to the highways at an alarming rate.) Some cycling clubs, of which Guildford Phoenix was a pioneer, form junior sections (age 12-15) in collaboration with the Road Safety and Youth Officers, both to assist with road safety and riding proficiency and also to encourage active interest in cycling as a sport. In May 1963 the Duke of Edinburgh attended a National Child Cycling Proficiency Rally held at the White Stadium, London, where he watched school-children ride over test courses to give a practical demonstration of the advantages of being taught to ride correctly under the proficiency scheme. Cycling plays its part also in the Duke of Edinburgh's Award scheme.

Since 1963 some schools, beginning with schools under the LCC, have added cycling to their curriculum, several providing coaching sessions during school time. Some have sought affiliation with the controlling body of the sport of cycling, Foxwood School, Leeds, being the first to do so. In certain areas, including East Anglia, there are now inter-school cycling leagues: in Scotland four schools use the Meadowbank track, Edinburgh, for competitive events. Currently, 1971, under the auspices of the British Cycling Federation, a Junior Star Trophy competition is being introduced, to stimulate interest in junior racing. In addition the BCF receives invitations to take part in the 'Semaine Européene' for young cyclists, a sporting tourist trial, now in its second year, held over five days in late July at Bois de Villers, Belgium. Young riders will have a chance to measure themselves against each other at a *home* international event to be staged at Skegness next year, sponsored by Butlins.

A programme which caters for most age groups and abilities has been developed recently via Hertfordshire Young Olympic Cycling Group. A well-known Olympic rider, supported by members of the local club, organises the training of enthusiastic boy riders at Welwyn stadium each weekend. Track and road work and gymnastic exercise are included in the course; during the summer at mid-week league meetings races for boys are held on the track. For those who achieve certain standards in the various events there are awards of Olympic rings. Although there is apathy in some quarters still, membership of ESCA (English Schools' Cycling Association) doubled in 1971.

Many clubs, of course, organise their own schoolboy events in such annuals as the RSPA cycling week, include junior club runs in their programme, and weekly club meetings with lectures on such cycling topics as maintenance and map reading. The junior response is often to turn out to watch senior club events at 7 o'clock on Sunday mornings! This goes some way at least to bridge the gap, specially mentioned in the Wolfenden Report on Sport, 1961, that may occur between leaving school and finding a vocation in an organised purposeful recreation. For the younger rider, *Cycling* carries regular features—such as a special springtime overhaul. Diagrams of wheels, brakes, handlebars, pedals, chainwheel, chain, gears, saddle, headset and bearings, and clear instructions as to testing and trueing up provide essential information both for safety and for the enjoyment of efficiency in the machine.

> 'Who is he? What does he do?'
> 'He works in a bicycle shop.'
> Bicycle shop consoled him. He was a common man—like

himself. Also he could discern a faint aura of ridiculousness attached to bicycles.

[Patrick Hamilton, *The Midnight Bell*, 1935]

The jealous admirer, in the novel, feels therefore no sense of inferiority (he is a waiter); perhaps even he feels the reverse. The 'common man' appeal is one which cyclists—like rock-climbers—would not disclaim, however much those whose transport depends on the combustion engine may at times affect to look down upon or regard him with faint amusement. Cycling, in its various forms, is an activity which makes for common ground between all manner of men—whether Minister of Transport, like the Rt Hon Ernest Marples (an enlightened user of a hand-built lightweight), who when in office took his wife for a cycling tour on the Riviera, or sons of the mining and industrial districts of the north, like Reg Harris or the late Tom Simpson, who established his racing fame there.

A great feature of the association of cyclists from the start has been its inclusiveness. 'The CTC is more than a club—more even than a national organisation. It is a family of friends.' Although the former club slogan, 'CTC for Happy Cycling', is not nowadays backed by the weight of numbers that it once enjoyed, the organisation seems to do more than ever for its members. From the year of the club's majority, 1899, when membership reached over 60,000 and it was the 'done thing' to belong, membership settled down to comprise those whose need and appreciation of the bicycle were greater, but funds usually less. (When it was proposed to raise the standard subscription for 1959 to 30s, fear that membership might fall to 27,000 kept it then at 25s.) For whatever kind of cyclist the club offered more than just insurance and travel concessions, legal aid and local advice, in the form of activities making for good companionship at all stages.

'An organisation for the formation of friendship', the CTC claims to provide a place for everyone. The gap for adolescents is bridged here on a wider basis than in the purely competitive sporting field.

149

There *are* special trials arranged for young cyclists, map-reading events, hill climbs, free-wheeling contests, 'rough stuff' expeditions, and the less serious types of competition such as treasure hunts. There are also standard rides of 50 miles in four hours, 100 in seven, eight or nine, 220 or 250 miles in twenty-four hours and so on, in which juniors at times take part with notable success, even at the adult distances. These may lead to the 'tourist trials', including tests and questionnaires of the type employed in the British Cycle Tourist Competition, the most comprehensive of national cycling contests. One or two of the northern district associations hold, in addition, a 10,000ft event in which a large number of heights are covered in the course of eight hours' riding.

But a wider variety of activity than these helps to link young with older members, hard-riders with loiterers. The regular club runs—the mainstay of the District Association programme—go much beyond a mere 'getting in the miles'. Visits to local places of interest are arranged, ancient trackways and Roman roads are rediscovered, sites of battle and legend traced. The National Trust properties, private estates open to the public under the National Gardens scheme, old castles, new reservoirs, atomic power stations —all provide a change of focus. Mystery trips, 'change leader' and 'first left, first right' runs add the lighter side; and, in common with clubs like the Anfield which have 'autumn tints' and other seasonal fixtures, the DA's programme will include night rides (at full moon), 'nut runs', holly runs and, in summer, swimming and boating runs. In club rooms, as well as the usual social events, photographic competitions, colour slide evenings and talks by members revive highlights and provide a foretaste of events in the CTC year.

The fear that 'settling down' will inevitably put an end to cycling is groundless. Relationships formed through the CTC often lead to partnerships in life—one Surrey section recorded twenty-seven marriages between its own members in a period of ten years. Although cycling may have to take second place to home-making at first, the return to active membership is consistently encouraged. At such events as the CTC Annual Rally, in addition to grass-track events and trade exhibitions, camp craft and cycle polo, there is certain to be a 'family trophy', awarded to the best turn-out with tandems and sidecars to accommodate the contestants' additions. Not everyone can muster the enthusiasm to buy a quadruplet and construct a trailer behind it, in order to bring up a family of six awheel, but family cycling has enjoyed a minor boom in the last decade.

FOR THE CYCLIST WHO PRIDES THE BIKE HE RIDES—a display notice for a certain machine 'built by experts', may not be standard English but it communicates the enthusiasm of those who man and scrutinise the Cycle Show stands. Staged biennially at Earl's Court or, on northern occasions, at Blackpool, the show offers to the complete cyclist (and mopedaller) all that is new in machines, clothing, accessories and spares from one end of the price scale to the other. The young rider's under £20 machine, the shopping model for housewives, the 'best-you-can-buy' specification of racing team road machine, the novelty—such as the old Ordinary reproduced in a 40in wheel, with a safety device to prevent riders going over the top when the brake is applied, the 'expense-no-object' bicycle with immaculate components and flamboyant finish—these are some of the crowd magnets. Cotterless chainsets or pearl plastic mudguards, handlebar stop-watch clips or top-tube primus stove carrier, cutaway racing saddles or lightweight brake shoes—items for promoting ease of use, safety, speed or simply enhancing appearance, prove the fallacy of believing that any machine, however apparently perfect, is incapable of improvement. The show is the shop-window of the British Cycle Industries Association and attracts daily attendances in the order of twenty thousand, many of whom arrive on their bicycles.

When he has 'genned up' on frames and accessories, the real

cycling enthusiast—who takes a pride not only in the 'bike he rides', but in building it up himself with the latest components—turns naturally to clothing. The fashionable trends are as manifest in cycling as in climbing or other special-need sports. A clubman's spring outfit, for instance, might include a 'Le Paris' woollen sweater, Richelieu cotton stockings, Gran Sport black leather shoes, a Quelda plastic lightweight cape and grey whipcord shorts—to quote some practicable and comfortable garments with definite style of the late 1950s. Four or five years later the cyclist considering a summer outfit might choose between such items as an Adastra drip-dry jacket, white or navy sports shirt, cavalry twill shorts, tweed 'plus two's' or Italian terylene pantalons, bri-nylon socks, hand-made Italian shoes and perhaps the Alex touring cap. Protection from weather, ventilation, lightness, comfort are first considerations, but fashion sense comes a close second.

From Cycle Show to Camping and Outdoor Life Show is an obvious step for the complete cyclist. Today a rider's horizon can be as wide as his purse and leisure time permits. The cyclist who built up a lightweight racing machine to his own requirements—it could easily be folded up to carry by one hand—and with a pair of panniers and saddle bag, spare tyres, spokes, free-wheel springs and ratchets set off a few years ago to traverse fourteen countries on a cycle camping trip to the Himalayas is not necessarily the exception, but only the exceptionally privileged in opportunity. He carried a lightweight sleeping bag, small pressure stove and canteen, mosquito net, water sterilisation kit, a few medical items and then was independent: 'no bother with documents for cars, finding suitable places to park, or traversing difficult roads. . . . One can stop wherever one wishes with a bicycle, go slower so as to take in the surrounding sights, make a quieter approach to wild life, and enjoy those wonderful long descents through mountain roads, and at the same time keep fit with the exercise'.

The camping cyclist, whether or not he has Himalayan horizons in view, wants the most reliable, simple, light-and-strong equipment available. Tents with sewn-in groundsheet or with separate nylon groundsheet (with or without flysheet), weighing no more than 3½lb, butane or solid fuel cooker, inclusive kitchen sets or single items in spun aluminium, cycle trailers that weigh under 20lb and with loading capacity of over 100lb, one-man tents folding to pocket size and weighing under 2lb, special food items, multi-purpose knives and hatchets, down or Rhovyl-filled sleeping bags in drip-dry cotton or terylene: these are some of the types of equipment available that have removed lightweight camping from the era of 'living rough' into that of almost luxurious roving.

What, asked 'Kuklos' (Fitzwater Wray) in one of his papers, collected 1927, are the motives of those who persistently 'ride or wriggle on wheels'? The phrase was Ruskin's—occasioned by riders of high bicycles invading his Lakeland seclusion—and it provoked from Wray a list of the 'Thirty-Nine Articles of his Faith'. Among these were enjoyment of British roads, 'the best in the world'; of real bicycles 'no longer "push-bikes" '; of one's own power used as 'economically or prodigally as you please'; of keen competitive athletics in youth; of their incentive for the cultivation of good health; of the freemasonry of the road and the club; of exploration; and of the elements and seasons 'without a saloon body', and, because of the absence in cycling of noise, smell, fear or discomfort caused to other wayfarers. And, incidentally, as 'Kuklos' wryly observes, 'because convicts wear numbers but cyclists need not' and 'the bicycle brings its owner no demand note from the Inland Revenue on the first day of every year'.

The freemasonry of road and club, together with the prodigal or economical use of one's own power 'as you please', are cogent factors in keeping the mature (or the family cyclist) active and enthusiastic. Even when the interests of membership are mostly racing on road and track, as in the Catford CC up to its golden jubilee, non-racing events like utility rides of sixty or seventy miles make 'a day with the club' magnetic for others also. (In utilities no one knows where they have to go until they start, and at the first check riders learn the name of the next and so on—all checks being of ten minutes at well-known tea places, with a lunch check of forty-five minutes.) To help in keeping up attendances at club runs the rule, common in principle to most clubs, can be invoked that 'no member is eligible to receive a prize or medal unless he has attended at least twenty per cent of the club runs, all runs on the fixture list to count. A member competing in an open event in the club's name is entitled to score the club's run for that day'. Committees find it occasionally a necessary, if unpleasant duty, strictly to enforce this rule.

In case, as with some exclusive clubs, women feel out of the picture, organised cycling weekends for women have come into prominence since the fifties. A northern all-female event has drawn women cyclists from the whole country to Wortley Hall; corresponding events have from time to time been arranged in the Midlands, at Loughborough (for training) and in the south. Attendances of two hundred, at a time when the number of girls who cycle is decreasing, are testimony both to the desire of women not to lose their cycling fitness and keenness, from mere slavery to the kitchen sink, to their 'club-ability', and to their enjoyment of chances to explore unfamiliar terrain for themselves. The variety of appeal of these weekends—purely social, strictly training, or semi-family affairs—has been a key to their success.

The injunctions and advice on physical aspects, in the days of the Mowbray House cycling association for working girls and Rational Dress CA, already quoted (p95), showed women as indeed the 'cyclo-chrysalids' they were sometimes termed. 'How does it affect our health?' was then practically always the first question. To compare this with the pleas in the columns of *Cycling* and other such journals today for more entries by girl time trialists into local track league and BCF competition, as part of their roadman training with a view to finding the potential for world championship teams, is to make one realise how much cycling has helped to change women's outlook within only two generations. To go for a gruelling 'training bash' alongside brother, boy-friend or husband as pacer is now almost a *sine qua non* for success. Women have beaten the hour on 25s with scarcely more fuss than men on an out-and-home 100m have got inside the four. The factitious lure of speed, though a powerful drug, has seldom proved to be harmful.

It was bruited abroad, in the doubtful days of 1921, that among the causes of premature decease of a Yorkshire cycling club were the then bad state of the roads and the excessive motor traffic. In the early twenties there was hopeful talk of new road planning schemes, but for a long time authorities concentrated instead on widening and rectifying old roads: the AA and RAC erected numerous warning signs and provided 'scouts' as extra traffic police at difficult cross-roads. A cycling journal saw fit to assure its readers that there was not the slightest need for any club to cease operations or for any individual cyclist to be 'driven off the roads' because of the numerical presence of motor vehicles. Cyclists must attune themselves to the new road conditions and be prepared for a probable 'further increase in mechanically propelled vehicles in the next ten years'. Fifty years later, to the month, a contributor to the same journal reported counting, as he waited to turn out of a city thoroughfare into a side road, 'the number of cars racing up the slope, with bonnets practically touching rear fenders' and, excluding motor-cycles, he reached a level eighty in about as many seconds. That was between 5.30pm and 6.30pm on a weekday, the 'normal chaos where one important road crosses another or a roundabout brings fighters from many directions'. Cyclists made a brave if at times apprehensive showing. On the other hand, if one took the same journey at 8.0pm the lines of parked cars had practically vanished, it was possible to ride as close to the kerb as the single, double or treble yellow lines, and, when traffic lights changed from red, to move off immediately—instead of seeing red change to green but being still unable to pedal because crossing traffic was jammed.

For the complete cyclist, then, the traffic problem largely resolves itself into choice of time and choice of route. 'He always plans a route and ever one unknown to the Esso-mapped motoring fraternity.' He knows all the traffic-free lanes and only occasionally needs a map when 'development' has altered the once familiar landscape. Such cyclists acquire a wide acquaintance with British topography of their own esoteric kind. . . .

A more recent cause for complaint is that on some old green tracks, in perhaps Wales or the Derbyshire dales, where there were once only two cart ruts, there is now a third in the middle of the turf. Motor cyclists, in search of 'colonial courses' over unmetalled tracks in remoter parts of the countryside, are often responsible. By them, if not by the passage of tractors or tanks, too many of the ancient green roads—a cyclist's delight—are being ruined or endangered.

Apart from events in most club programmes for 'veterans' (qualifying age officially forty) and TTA groups exclusively veteran in Kent and London, in the Midlands, the West of England and the North there are ample opportunities for the middle-aged cyclist both to enjoy and serve his sport. In the writer's district, for instance, the active president of the Tricycle Association is well past sixty. Although it is sometimes a justifiable complaint that club committees tend to be overweighted with the over-forties, yet for their work and that of the organisers, time-keepers, trainers, fund-raisers, the unpaid 'soigneurs' there can hardly be excess of experience or of willingness to sacrifice leisure.

The 'fathers of the sport', unobtrusive men who retain their youth by encouraging youth, who pass on their own 'know-how', are, as cycling history shows, often the figures behind outstanding current champions. 'There is no better way of preparing for cycling than by cycling itself' may be true: but it is only part of the truth. Trial and error, which can consume so much of the potential of the novice, may be halved by the transmitted experience of the 'old guard'. It takes perhaps a Goodman ('Goz') of the French B/C team, son of a Goodman (Dick, past winner of the North Road 24), himself the son of a champion cyclist, to realise that in full. But whether they belonged to a pre-war 'Century Club', qualification 100 miles within five hours, or a 'Loiterers' section to roam the country lanes—with its steward in the rear calling out 'Oi!' whenever an infrequent motor car approached—these veterans invariably communicate infectious enthusiasm for their way of life.

HELMS.

"I wish you'd go a bit more slowly through these nice bits of scenery."

CHAPTER NINE

FOR PLEASURE AND PROFIT: RACING

RACING, RECORD-BREAKING and cycling have gone together from the start: races against the horse, against the human, team or individual, and against the clock. Record-breaking has been of the life-blood of most clubs, however 'social' their general aims. From earliest days such clubs as the Anfield have had their members' silver button, with a special narrow beaded edge for riders who earned it by some special record achievement. In internal and external events clubs have nurtured talent, kept up enthusiasm, and produced, like Kirkby CC, top internationals.

In the long-distance field standards for stars and medals like these, set up by the Anfield BC in 1885, helped to sort out the sheep from the goats. In a 24 hour run, from midnight to midnight, with no piece of road to be counted more than twice, a silver star was awarded for 100 miles on any machine; a gold star for 200 miles on either bicycle or tandem tricycle; for 175 miles on single tricycle a gold star. For the longest distance in any one day during the club year, on any machine, the award was a gold medal, and

*Racing man—A. W. Harris (Leicester), sometime holder of
the English mile record, on a Humber*

for any national long-distance record—over 100 miles on bicycle
or tandem tricycle, over 50 on single bicycle—which satisfied the
NCU—a gold medal.

Apart from internal contest series the Anfield, to use it as an
example, joined the other northern clubs to form a North Road
Club, founded in 1885 to provide more opportunities for racing in
and around the Great North Road, and linked it with a North Road

Record Association. The Road Records Association, of which the North Road Club, the Bath Road and other clubs were joint founders, was formed in 1888—the year that Dunlop patented his pneumatic tyre—and took over from the NCU the registration of road records when that body decided to confine its activities to the path. In 1898 unpaced road records were established (prior to that riders took advantage of what pacing they could get) after the introduction by F. T. Bidlake of time trials to replace massed-start road racing which had been discontinued. The first of the time trial events run by the North Road Club at 50 miles, was held in October 1895.

The 'End-to-End' (Land's End to John o' Groats), earliest of all the long-distance records—though strictly it was place-to-place—was recognised both by clubs and by the public well before road record committees took cognisance of it. Times established in the 1870s on Ordinaries over the estimated distance of 800 miles, which came down from over a fortnight to just over eleven days, were almost halved in 1884-5 by a number of riders until Anfielder George Mills knocked the bottom out of the Ordinary record with a time of 5 days 1hr 45min in 1886. Other place-to-place records in early days were classed in comparison with mail coach times—GPO London to York or Liverpool in about 20 hours. An Anfielder, D. R. Fell, covered the 201 miles from club base Liverpool to London, in April 1885, in just ten minutes over the twenty hours riding time, within the club rules of midnight to midnight.

Other clubs, of course, have their prominent place in the promotion of distance records or other types of event. The SCCU, formed by fourteen southern counties' clubs including the Catford, the Oval and the Tooting in 1898 when the SRRA was dissolved, fostered both road and track competition, and was justifiably regarded as the great provider of the racing man's needs. As the road course is halfway to Brighton (Brighton-and-back being the 'classic' of the place-to-place rides) clubs as far away as

Portsmouth have enjoyed membership and shared in featuring road and track promotions on SCCU's behalf. Their early time trials include a 'memorial' '100', and a hill climb. The Good Friday track meetings at Herne Hill, or less frequently at Paddington or Portsmouth, have attracted the 'great'—from Leon Meredith of Paddington CC, who 'came back' in 1924 at the age of forty-two to beat long-standing 100 miles figures, to Frank Southall of Norwood Paragon, dominant from the twenties to the thirties, a professional for Hercules. (Top time trialists were eagerly 'signed up' by the rival manufacturing companies, which both helped to produce the stimulating road record rivalry of the thirties and, with the publicity on racing successes, helped to sell bicycles and sustain exports.) For outstanding talent at the Hill the early trophies were as outstanding. The Penrose Cup, won outright by Meredith in 1909, weighed 209oz and held eight gallons. To fill it up in winner's traditional style would have cost then 10s 8d, good beer being sold at twopence a pint. Sixty years after its formation the SCCU was providing racing for well over a hundred clubs.

In America bicycle racing had a large, enthusiastic following from the 1880s and Arthur Zimmerman's heyday up to the end, in 1961, of the era of the six-day race in Madison Square Gardens, said at one time to attract more spectators than any other sport. Successful racers, whether in national road championships or 'Velodrome' events, have been the American sports heroes of their day: their demands for lighter and faster machines have accelerated many manufacturers' improvements; their associations, the former NCA and the ABL, have had, like their British counterparts, their share of errors of promotion and control. The names of Murphy, 'Zim', Marshall Taylor, of Tyler, Sanger, Windle (of the Springfield Club), McDougal, Marcus Hurley and Frank Kramer, best-ever American sprinter and world champion in 1912, have their historic place. The Madisons or 'jams' involved a degree of teamwork in pick-ups and skill in weaving through traffic which long excited

K

enthusiastic admiration. Today promotion costs, the heavy demand on all arenas for professional basketball and ice hockey and the general preference by Americans for sports enjoyable in shorter bursts, have left only two professional riders in the USA, while those who wish to watch indoor cycle racing must go across the border to Montreal.

AGAINST THE WATCH

The sport of bicycle racing, as the foregoing will suggest, has three main divisions: time trial, track race and massed-start road race. The first, the 'race of truth', an essentially British form of sport, involves an individual only and a watch—*contre la montre* as the continental term has it. Track racing, which in the bicycle's boom day became pre-eminent, now forms the smallest segment of the sport: the costs of stadia and the need for paying crowds impose their limits, in such a competitive field as popular spectacle. Massed-start racing, the national sport of Belgium, France and Italy, involving many men in almost gladiatorial battles of will, stamina and wits, has made a come-back in Britain after its earlier demise. The English 'tiger' abroad and the foreign champion in English events have now become familiar figures, with a good deal of seasonal fanfare. To understand the 'scene' and the social adaptations it will be advantageous to consider each division of the sport separately.

Since the first time trial '50' run by the NRCC these events have been regulated first through liaison with the Road Racing Council, formed in 1922 by a group of clubs to ensure uniformity in conduct of trials, then nationally by its successor, the Road Times Trial Council, since 1938. The latter has no direct members but takes a small levy from race entries, and from the club fees of affiliated clubs. In order to enjoy the use of the public highway with less disturbance to and from the public, in view of earlier road race troubles, both the location and the time of the start for individual events were divulged to entrants only. Memories of the attitude at the beginning of time trials, that a machine ridden at 20mph was a menace to the community, no doubt assisted in maintaining this secrecy during the RTTC's first twenty-five years of regulation. The various courses were indicated by key numbers and the date by numbers referring to weekends throughout the year. Post-event publicity in the press remained vague and it was each rider's responsibility to prevent the name of his machine appearing in any newspaper photograph; preliminary press notices specifying riders or clubs participating were completely banned.

In order to obtain favourable conditions, to avoid traffic as much as possible and, of course, to separate these activities from normal public road use, events started at 5.0am or even 4.0am in the height of the summer. Code numbers for more than seven hundred courses are still used, but since 1963 secrecy has been waived—mainly in order to attract youngsters to the sport. There are many events solely for the club members' own enjoyment—short, mid-week evening runs or those early on Sunday morning, such as the writer has often watched across the green levels of Cambridgeshire and Lincolnshire, where pre-war riders in their black alpaca jackets and black tights would carve painfully into the wind the hard leg of their 25 or 50 miles and then swoop back downwind like hawks diving to the kill. The rest are area or 'open' events, open that is to the different categories of rider, with cups, plaques, vouchers and certificates as the usual prizes.

Riders are classed either as amateurs, who neither compete for gain nor with 'independents' and 'pros' and are not permitted to make a profit in connection with cycling; aspirants, who while conforming to the amateur definition in other ways are allowed for not more than one year to ride against independents and professionals; independents, who take prizes and are unable to revert to amateur status, holding an independent licence for up to two years

163

whilst preparing for professionalism; the professionals, who make a career of cycling and are free to capitalise in any way financially. By the rules certain events are open to two or more categories, but amateurs must not compete with any other class than amateur or aspirant, if they are to maintain their status.

The variety of time trial events—short at 10, 15, 20 or 30 miles, middle at 50 and 100, long-distance 12 and 24hr—caters for men, women and novices. The season begins at the end of February with 25s for hard riders and medium gear (maximum 72in) 25s to offset wintry weather and lowered standards of fitness. The real stuff starts at Easter with the 50s; early 100s come in at Whitsuntide, while 12hr events and over predominate in July and August. The 'Blue Riband' events—the Bath Road Club 100 mile (first won, in 1890, by Edmund Dangerfield the founder of *Cycling*)—are timed for August Bank Holiday. At the end of the season shorter events and hill climbs take place: a traditional 25 miles is run on Christmas Day. Veterans, tricyclists, 'middle-markers', first-class riders are all catered for in suitable 'opens' in an annual programme containing well over a thousand events.

National championships, instituted by the RTTC, have formed part of this programme since 1944. They begin in early June, when 'form' has been established by both men and women, and go on to the men's 24hr event at the end of August, then to hill climbs in October. A most coveted amateur title, British Best All Rounder (a competition inaugurated by *Cycling* in 1930), gives added meaning and tension to the season's events. Competitors from England, Scotland and Wales with the best average speed in specified 50 mile, 100 mile and 12hr events compose the field for this. Many time trial courses have tended to go flat in recent years in order to obtain good BAR results.

Time trials exert appeal long after most speedmen have hung up their 'sprints' for good. A rider, for example, who first tried his hand at the game when he was twenty-six, 'Arch' Harding of

Middlesex Road Club, and gained a measure of fame by finishing second in the Westerley RC '100' a year or two later, went on to win the Bath Road Cup outright, with three wins at the age of thirty-three. Twelve years later, riding in the same event, he was able to record a time within two seconds of his best figure—4hr 17min 46sec—when he had made competition history by being the first man to win inside 4hr 20min. The following year, 1959, Harding made a remarkable first attempt at a 24hr trial, by way of giving a final knock to the already outworn theory of 'too old at forty' for racing. In time trials the scientific approach, a calculating brain allied to developed cycling physique and accumulated knowledge, can do wonders to offset loss of youthful vigour. Harding's favourite gear was 81in fixed: his ability to pedal rather than push, to surmount hills without loss of rhythm, to 'ankle' into wind, to 'fly' on down grades using rather than fighting prevailing conditions, to hold back his effort while others went thundering past, never riding all out until confident that his reserves could last to the end, brought a long list of successes.

The tale could be repeated. L. W. Mills, for instance, at fifty-three rode his fourth and best trial in the Manchester and District 12hr with 226½ miles in persistent rain.... Many experienced time trialists have preferred the fixed single instead of variable gears even on gradients, as an aid to rhythm when taking part in middle-distance events. In 12 and 24hr events a set of gears, such as 90-84-79-74-66, might be adopted. The fashion for the single chain wheel, although 5 speed gears came back into favour even in the fifties, has continued: a thrusting trialist on a flattish course would push 112-97-91in ratios.

By the Cycle Racing on Highways regulations (1960) the organising secretary of any club promoting road events is required to provide details in writing to the appropriate chief officer of police twenty-eight days before an event. If the course that is proposed crosses county boundaries it is essential to obtain authority from all chief constables involved, or the trialist may find himself being stopped. Normally no more than 120 riders are allowed in 'opens' up to 50 miles, 100 riders in other events and in association fixtures 150. By RTTC rules station marshals must be appointed to man the course posts and the starting interval between competitors must not be less than one minute. In team trials the teams, of not more than four riders, start at intervals of not less than five minutes, with not more than twenty-four in any event. Riding must normally be in single file—always so when passing a vehicle—with only the minimum amount of echelon to allow view ahead. If one team overtakes another the onus is on the team overtaken to drop back . . . these conditions both preserve the event's characteristics, avoid irresponsible racing and cut the ground for other road users' complaints of inconvenience. That key figure, the timekeeper, must have both watch, certified by the British Horological Institute, and appropriate assistance.

Prior to World War II competitive cycling for women, especially over long distances, received little encouragement or support. The efforts of Lilian Dredge, both as rider and official—she personally put the End-to-End (872m) record 'on the book' for the WRRA and was the first English girl to compete in a Continental road race (1934)—helped notably in breaking through this attitude. For women subsequently time trials have supplied new 'vital statistics'. The remarkable 'golden girl' of post-war cycling, in the decade after Eileen Sheridan (who also became a professional for Hercules), found herself classified as 24½-23¾-23¼—the round speed of her record performances at 25 miles, 50 miles and 100 miles respectively. This girl, Beryl Burton, of Morley CC, after winning every women's national time trial championship, with an improved time on each occasion, including 4hr 18min 19sec in the revised Bath '100' on an 84in fixed gear and making competition records at 12hr, restored a British name to the list of world road champions for the first time in almost forty years. She won not only the 1960 world pursuit title at 3,000 metres on the track for the second time, but the same week in Germany took the 38-mile road world championship with a time of 1hr 54min 39sec and a lead of 3min 37sec over her nearest rival. The fifth, sixth and seventh laps were, for Beryl Burton, pure time trialing by a mistress of that art. Two years later, in Milan, she won back the pursuit title from a Belgian challenger and in doing so beat the 'four minute barrier' with a time of 3min 59.4sec, the first ride by a woman within the four minutes. In addition to her world champion rainbow jerseys and four Best British All Rounder awards Mrs Burton, riding in an Easterley RC '25', became in May 1963 the first woman to 'beat the hour', recording a time of 59min 25sec—and without being able to get top gear of the range of five! Then, in three successive years, 1967, 8, 9, she broke the 12 hour, 4 hour and 2 hour 'barrier' respectively for women, for 275 miles, 100 and 50 miles. Between whiles, since 'racing isn't everything' she enjoys cycle-camping.

For road record breaking under control of the Road Records Association—the place-to-place routes referred to above and distances such as 1,000 miles—a major factor to be considered is the meteorological forecast and wind direction. For an attack on major road records, such as the 'End-to-End', long-range weather forecasts as provided by the American Institute of Aerological Research (Zurich) are sought in order to try to ensure a flying start—a strong tail wind of perhaps 20mph. Successful time trialists at the peak of form, usually with the backing of cycle manufacturers, may then make a bid which, if successful, will establish the rider as a giant of the sport. A time-keeper, appointed by the RRA, 'credible witnesses' or checkers from clubs en route, and a posse of helpers with their following vehicles, feeding and repair facilities, perhaps also a medical adviser, plus police co-operation in towns traversed, make these ambitious undertakings in all senses.

When, for example, David Duffield regained the 'End-to-End' tricycle record in 1960, he started from Land's End one July morning before a sweeping south-west wind, forecast in March for the approximate few days' period. After sixteen hours' riding, however, the wind changed to a nagging head wind and frequent showers, so that by Carlisle the rider, tired of struggling into it, threatened retirement unless there was hope of a change. A weather forecast, later to prove false, was passed to him promising a following wind later in the day. He forged on, and into torrential rain in Scotland, to cut 1hr 39min off the previous record for a 'barrow' (tricycle) and to reach John o' Groat's in 2 days 10hr 58min. Ten-speed gears, high-pressure tyres, freedom from mechanical fault, peak fitness and a rigorous training programme are not in themselves enough to create conditions for success in major undertakings like this, essential as they all are.

IN THE STADIUM

Racing on the track, once the popular crowd magnet, has felt the wind of change: in default of sufficient capital to 'splash' events where the great majority of the competitors are amateur, it has enjoyed restricted support since World War II but continues to attract its hundreds of enthusiasts. It requires not only special conditions, special equipment and techniques of training, but in order to enjoy it fully a special knowledge in spectators alert to its complexities.

The special cement, asphalt or tarmac tracks number about two dozen in Britain in general or occasional use. Apart from the traditional homes of track racing at Herne Hill and Paddington, London, at the Butts, Coventry and Fallowfield Stadium (run for a period by Reg Harris) in Manchester, there are hard tracks in Birmingham, Brighton, Portsmouth, Wolverhampton, Cardiff (one of the best), Cannock and other cities, supplemented in the north by shale and cinder tracks. Grass-track racing also has its following and championships under British Cycling Federation rules. The Good Friday meeting at Herne Hill opens the season; nearly all centres have Whitsuntide meets; Manchester Wheelers' meet, in July, is the chief northern event; Herne Hill closes the season with the meeting of champions. As well as being venues for national championships (twelve for men, three for women, usually staged at Coventry, Manchester or in London), tracks are in regular use for the league weekly meetings, open to all clubs affiliated with the BCF which was formed to cover both track and road racing in 1959.

There are four main classes of track race: the short-distance—¼ or ½ mile—'explosive' events, pursuit and distance races, and paced events. In classic match sprints only two riders compete; as a race 'three up' is better to watch. In the amateur sprint, aristocrat of the track races, the sequence of British world domination in the event, which had been broken after World War I, was re-asserted by Reg Harris in 1947. He also won two silver medals in the London Olympics, 1948, and when he turned professional, for Raleigh, went on to win four world sprint titles (see plate, p126). In 1954 the world amateur sprint title came to Britain also, via Cyril Peacock; and to make it a British decade Norman Shiel won the world amateur pursuit race in both 1955 and 1958 (see plate, p144). Promoters' fees paid to a professional world champion appearing at subsequent track meetings range from £80 to £100.

Pursuit racing, a most exciting test of speed, stamina, courage and judgement, is run at speeds up to 30mph over 4,000m or 5,000m, for team or individual. Starters are placed at equidistant positions round the track, each then attempting to overtake the one in front and avoid being overtaken, which enforces retirement. Together with distance racing this style complements the sprint. The distance events come in various guises—'unknown', 'devil-take-the-hindmost' or 'miss, an' out' (in which the last rider is eliminated at each lap or half lap), 'omnium', 'point-to-point'—scoring variously at lap end and race finish, 'course de primes' and 'madison'—American in name and tradition as a six-day event with riders in pairs, one racing, one resting, entitled to relieve each other at any time.

Paced events are crowd compellers. Between the wars tandem-paced races were the height of popularity at Herne Hill: since then motor-cycle pacing with 1,000cc machines roaring round the track at 50mph have taken the gilt. German tracks such as Leipzig's afford scope for this at world class; Britain lacks the small, ultra-smooth and steeply-banked tracks which are necessary, although events are run at various venues including Wembley and Dublin. A pacing bike requires straight front forks; the distance from bottom bracket to front-wheel spindle must be 35cm.

A typical Whitsuntide international meeting of the kind held at the Harris stadium, Fallowfield, under BCF rules could include the following events: an 'all-star' international amateur sprint at 550yd, with a world sprint champion appearance—first prize (value) £10; an international omnium in three-match races; the three-mile point-to-point; one-mile record attempt from a standing start; and a five-mile motor-paced race; the world professional sprint championship 'revenge series' in three matches; a 4,000m individual pursuit race first prize (value) £6; a professional 'devil'; the quarter-mile flying start record attempt (to beat Harris's own record time of 24sec); finally, an amateur international five miles, first prize (value) £10 and a professional international trophy race, point-to-point over 15 miles with its special sprint laps. Under the rules any rider suffering a mechanical defect or puncture was allowed up to a maximum of two laps in which to rejoin the race, providing that there were more than three laps remaining to complete it. From the spectator's viewpoint the elements here of expertise, drama, excitement would seem sufficient enough in themselves. But, at the date of writing, a sub-committee of the British Cycling Federation is considering the possibilty of bringing betting to the cycling track—in order to bring a new surge of interest to the sport, and looking especially towards the six-day events, reintroduced in 1967, on the principle that 'the louder the trumpets blare the better the public likes it.' Perhaps we shall see a revival of the *'Vél 'd'Hiv'* days in Paris (*Vélodrome d'Hiver*) where the midnight spectacle of the six-day cycle race was an extraordinary crowd-compeller, and after the recent successful Skol 6 series at Wembley's Empire Pool develop another indoor track.

For the sprinter who aims at the top, equipment is a prime consideration. Special clothing, styled and adapted to his needs, may make the difference in getting the best out of himself on the track. Sprint shoes, with ¼in soles and no artificial stiffening, that cling to the rider's feet like a pair of kid gloves; no socks—in order to avoid any risk of the foot slipping inside the shoe; legs shaved and oiled; skin-tight wool-cashmere shorts, with a chamois lining, cut lower in front than at the back of the waist and with no overlapping in seams or joins; a fine wool undervest of good body length and with quarter sleeves to absorb perspiration and keep away chills; a long cashmere, wool, or, if preferred, silk jersey of crew-neck design to fit wrinkle-free; the lightest chamois mitts and a 'crash-hat'—six bars of sponge-filled patent leather. These may give the wearer that critical one-tenth of a second.

There are certain basic principles in sprint machines for the best unification with the rider's body—or 'bikengine' as some racing trainers regard it. The handlebars, generally of about chest width, must not be too low, in order to avoid strain on the back muscles vital in producing the 'jump' which so often determines a close race; the angle of the grips must be calculated to obviate wrist cramp, occurring when too much weight is placed on the heel of the hand; the precise height of the saddle and its distance behind or in front of the bracket must be 'tuned' to the individual; the stronger his arms and shoulders the farther back the saddle may be for sprinting, the stronger and shorter his back the farther forward the saddle. To blend machine and rider into a perfect speed union means avoiding all strains and tendencies to wobble. In the final analysis that which produces results for the individual is, of course, the right riding position.

Among the hand-built 'hardware' the choice of a frame and its angles, of rims, of tyres (silk tubulars or 'tubs'), of saddle, of pedals, of chainwheel sets, of cranks, of hubs and of handlebars will be as wide as the most fastidious rider's demands to suit his needs, and as fine in quality as his purse commands. Carlton 'pro' frame sets, 1970, for instance go up to £26.25, Claude Butler £26 'ex-works', while offering along with Ellis Briggs, Harry Quinn, Freddie Grubb and other 'small' specialist makers, British, French and Italian, a reasonable range at competitive prices. A complete machine 'hand-built in our own workshops' with the latest French and Italian components may be £130 or more.

In order to enable the British rider to compete on equal terms with the Continental in the various forms of cycling sport, discriminating dealers now import a selection of the best-known models, as well as components. Such, for example, from the Jacques Anquetil range, as the 'Maillot Jaune' with its ultra-light Reynolds 531 tubes, solid-forged V-embossed fork crown and its fork ends forged with the rear incorporating a universal gear-arm bracket and built-in adjusters: or from the hand-built André Bertin range for beginner, course amateur, course competitor, course super professional and course *piste*, the course super-professional as ridden by Hoban and Holmes and tested on the *pavé* of northern France and Belgium, the so-called 'Hell of the North': or from the Cino Cinelli range, with frames individually made to order and 'produced up to a standard not down to a price', the model Pista for pursuit and track—an extra stiff frame giving no 'whip' in sprints, with reinforcing 'tangs' on the upper fork blades, head tube rifled as well as butted, solid seat lugs and parallel 73 head and seat angles. Again, Zeus *bicicletas especiales*, the Spanish marque used at the Mexico Olympiad, offer distinguished machines for *principante*, *aficionado* and professional, distinctively finished in Toledo copper

with white panels . . . The mystique of top-class racing machines
and the various minutiæ which may or may not win championships
are ventilated in the *Coureur* monthly magazine for the sporting
cyclist.

'There are few things finer in cycling than the sight of a good
pursuit team going flat out, each man working as part of the team.
There's something satisfying, too, in riding to catch an opponent on
the other side of the track. Yes, I definitely like pursuiting best of
all.' The opinion is that of Dave Marsh, for so long Britain's only
'golden roadman'. Many top riders have said that the individual
pursuit is the hardest race in the book—as much a battle of nerves
as a match sprint race and, because of its distance, 4,000m,
physically more exhausting. To match one's opponent and expend
only the effort needed to push one's bicycle over the finishing line
first is one way of riding it. To ride flat out the whole distance
with acceleration at the end, treating the race as a species of time
trial, is another. The pursuiter must develop a maximum pedalling
rate that he can reach as quickly as possible and maintain over
the whole distance, crouched in stream-lined position with his back
nearly parallel to the top tube. When he reaches his maximum the
only way that he can go faster, subsequently, is by increasing his
gear ratio and by using slightly longer cranks to help to keep the
gear rolling. This tests even top riders, such as Hugh Porter, in a
way beyond that of sprint racing.

In sprints the factors of tactical surprise and advantage, particularly in 'three up' sprints, are almost as important as pure speed.
The race 'from the front' is occasionally successful; the race from
second place, weaving or spreading so as to keep the third man
behind, or switching position up the banking to baulk his attack,
and then attacking in the home straight from the shelter of the first
man's wheel, is the more usual gambit. The gamble from third
place, by techniques such as 'taking a flyer' from the top of the
banking down across his rivals on the flat and making a rocket-like

173

'jump' to gain inside position, is a sample of tactics, possible only to past masters like Harris or Van Vliet, which no tyro with speed alone, of whatever calibre, can hope to match. The top-class sprinter masters each track and knows its foibles—such as the length of the finishing straight and the distance to the 200m mark after the first banking—studies his rivals and mentally dockets every one of their qualifications, racing methods and weaknesses, then with a worked out plan to win depends on the 'killer instinct' on the track itself to inspire reactions that will lead to victory. 'You must know how good you are,' was Reg Harris's view, 'but it is fatal to think that you are better than you are.'

There is no democratic sport today in which the pure amateur spirit is so predominant as in unpaced road competition. Whilst the Veteran Time Trial Association and the Tricycle Association may be regarded as the last two impregnable citadels of amateurism, the sport as practised under the code of the RTTC is fundamentally non-professional in slant. Here for the great majority the 'pleasure principle' operates. Where the profit principle is the operative one for the cycling careerist minority—out of an estimated ten million bicycles 'rolling' in Britain, perhaps one million are styled for sport, but only about ten thousand riders take part in serious competition, half of them in road racing and of these barely 1¼ per cent are 'pros'—the question comes up of massed-start road racing or track racing. The time trialist is used to sustained hard riding, solitary effort, self-judged pace; the trackman needs faster reactions, quick thinking, a very high power output for a short period only. For the 'roadman' some mixture of both is required—staying power and sudden dash capability: the aggressive, attacking rider is likely to get most out of it both in satisfaction and prizes. Which type of racing is tougher as a career?

'Big time' stage or long-distance single-day road racing, with the punishing hills, dust, heat, cold, rain, wind, endless miles of all-out effort and brutal demands on stamina and combative instinct, would seem unquestionably to be the harder option. But the roadman's hardihood is exercised in the context of a season of from six to eight months only; his professional activity is among team mates, his training requirements can be met partly by actual racing, once he has reached optimum fitness, and he is able to enjoy periods of complete relaxation. The trackman endures less muscle fatigue, but, if he is to stay at the top, can seldom afford to relax, and if he intends to hold his public must be prepared to race all the year round. Irrespective of his racing he must train assiduously, at or even above the level of competitive effort, often alone. He works to a fine schedule of gradients and speeds, for which he must await suitable track and weather conditions; if he goes over his fine limits, in an effort to make up for lost training time, he may succeed only in lowering his racing condition. His life, in fact, is regimented, his concentration unremitting: his speciality, whether sprint or pursuit racing, has to be kept at razor-edge keenness, despite participation in the 'madisons', omniums, six-day races and other money spinners required by the promoter.

ON THE ROAD

Massed-start road racing in this country was confined to closed circuits, such as those at Brooklands, the Crystal Palace, Donnington, until it could emerge from its period of internment after the NCU ban. British riders, for all their experience in solo effort and circuit event, were unable to make the grade in the open road type of continental race. During and after World War II the British League of Racing Cyclists carried out an intensive crusade for road racing on highways. The amateur Tour of Britain, sponsored by a daily newspaper, was begun in 1951; but road racing did not receive official NCU support for another three years. The first and rather premature appearance of a full British team in the classic Tour de France came in 1955 with the backing of the Hercules

Company. Two of the team finished the race, one as '*lanterne rouge*' or tail-light Charley—last on general classification—often a very popular figure as the rider who obviously can't win but won't give up. In 1959, in order to regularise the situation, the British Cycle Federation was formed, covering both road and track racing as well as representing Britain in the Olympic Association and in the Commonwealth Games Association. The following year Mrs Burton took her world road championship title.

What has become known as the 'Milk Race' since the Milk Marketing Board took over the Tour of Britain in 1955—their publicity aim being to sell more milk to young people via the athlete's appreciation—does much to groom British cyclists for continental events, not least by attracting other national teams into competition here. The trophy and prize (value) money—a total of £1,000 in early days rapidly increased three- or four-fold as the tours went on and further sponsors came in—and the growing prestige of this national summer sporting event encouraged roadmen to make it the axis on which their season revolved. Individual prizes come in values of £15 or £20 for stages, £5 for 'primes', prizes for aggression and special town prizes, and, for the tour winner, initially £100. Prize vouchers help the ablest roadmen to keep up their standard of mount in the highly specialised market of such components as Campagnolo hubs, Mafac brakes, Pirelli tubulars, Ambrosio bar sets, Raleigh professional frames; of Sun professional frame sets, Huret 'svelto' gears, Weinmann brakes and rims, Zeus chainsets; or, again, of Clive Stuart professional road and predator track sets, Cinelli bars, Milremo rims, Vittorio tubulars. The rider can only be as good as his mount.

In the opinion of some continental entrants the Tour of Britain was tougher than the Tour de France, with nearly as long stages, as hard and hazardous mountain stages, frightening descents through tight, busy little villages, difficult traffic conditions (with official penalties for breaches of road discipline) and, more significant, amateur contestants. Professional riders, as in France, bring balance to a race: they know when to go and when they must rest. Among amateurs, even after the hardest day, there is always someone willing and eager to 'have a go', which means therefore a race in which no rider can ever let up. Some discouragement of other national competitors, in fact, was experienced on certain courses selected for the Milk Race because of the gruelling mountain work in the first two days. In 1960, for example, both the Dutch contingent and the Swiss retired at less than halfway in the 1,500 miles, 14-day race, and the Belgians went after the sixth day, leaving only the Swedish team, among the continentals, in the race. The 'Milk for Stamina' tour clearly was frightening off those not willing to sacrifice season-long form in a race whose first stage switchbacked 114 miles from Blackpool to Morecambe via Pen-y-ghent, and whose second stage, 133 miles from Morecambe to Whitley Bay, crossed England's mountain backbone—six climbs, varying between ten and four miles in length, going up to 2,200ft, including a gradient of 1 in 3½ and some gated roads. This stage was won by W. Bradley, Southport, the previous year's winner, who won two of the mountain 'primes' (a bounty for winners of given sections, often used as spectator attraction) and was to go on in masterful style to win the tour also.

The course was altered. (The Tour de France also has been trimmed down—by 1,000 miles since 1928—and re-tailored.) The following year's race was much more open and allowed an extra day to cover the circuit. With the task of permuting stage towns with sufficient accommodation for the riders, routes acceptable to the police, places that fitted in with the Milk Marketing Board's publicity campaign, the organisers accepted the need to select terrain that would give every rider a fair chance. Their new tour headed south on the first day: the Morecambe-Whitley Bay stage, reversed in direction, came when the riders had been able to find their legs, next to the last stage. There was a first 'King of the

L

Mountains' tussle in the sixth stage, after 555 miles, between Cheltenham and Swansea by way of preparation, for which the Industries Association provided £500 in prize values. Any prize winner, however, whether on stages, mountains or points, could only receive his award if he completed the full course. A wider distribution of prizes and the withdrawal of definite time limits encouraged the lesser lights as well as the few supreme roadmen to keep going in an event which depends for its successful continuance on regional and service team entries as well as national.

The jerseys, the track suits and the MMB overalls, the shining brown legs, the glittering bicycles and the strange lettering, the foreign tongues, the gestures and the grimaces, the last minute testing of the gears, and the blowing up of tyres, the revving of engines and the clatter of shoe plates, all go to create the authentic atmosphere of a big sporting occasion. Only BFC regulations prevent the advertising on clothing or equipment in true continental style.

The scene is set: team managers are presented with bouquets, a helicopter cruises overhead, there are loud-speaker announcements, music from a military band. Then at 10.30 or 11.00 on a Whit-Sunday or Monday morning the flag is lowered and the gun fired. Through the controlled maelstrom of tanning holiday crowds, over the tramlines, between the Tower and the golden sands, down the road to Preston the tour sets off. No one can get out quickly enough: the pack heaves and bobs and rolls, followed by repair cars, ambulance and 'sag wagon'.

Within twenty miles, perhaps, there is real action, a group fighting to increase a two hundred yard lead, which, too good a break to be allowed to succeed, ends at 25 miles. . . . On to Nottingham, the longest stretch, pancake flats to Southend, the environs of London and its enthusiastic spectators; Hove, the coast road to traffic-littered, wind-battered Southsea, Bournemouth, Cheltenham: three climbs en route to Swansea, another five within seventy miles —including the Devil's Staircase (1 in 3)—from there to Aberyst-

178

wyth; then to Buxton, a 142 mile stage with two climbs in it; another four days (Skegness, Scarborough, out-and-home 25 mile time trial, Whitley Bay) before the 'primes' come in again with six mountain challenges through the Pennines, and hill descents hurtling at 45mph plus; on to Morecambe, with a final seventy miles into the last desperate sprint down Blackpool's thronged promenade. The bunch comes in—the labouring 'peloton' that has sorted itself out from the rest, with one man—the 'rouleur' who can go fast on the flat for miles, the phenomenal climber, the adequate time trialist, the more than adequate sprinter, the avoider or fortunate survivor of crashes—points ahead of the rest in stage wins, and daily placings, in short the race's master spirit. His garland of laurel has been well earned . . . his machine has proved over and over again its class.

The Tour de France event was launched nearly fifty years earlier than the Milk Race, in 1903, sponsored by Paris newspapers *L'Equipe* and *Le Parisien Libéré*. The 'trade team' idea operated for a generation before it was replaced by one of national type from 1930 for a similar period. When the tour was resumed after World War I the famous 'maillot jaune' or yellow jersey first appeared. Some of the stages then were so long—up to 300 miles—and the post-war roads in such a bad state that only eleven riders finished the course. The rider who finished last from the premature British team entry of 1955, Hoar of Emsworth, was 6hr 5min 37sec down on the time of the winner, for the third consecutive time, Louison Bobet: but the fact that he and Robinson finished at all made British cycling history. That was the challenge of this race.

Five years later a newly turned English professional, Simpson of Doncaster, member of a British national eight-man team, came very near to donning that symbol of race leadership, the yellow jersey, with second place on general classification, only 22sec down, at the end of the second stage, Brussels to Dunkirk. He went on to finish 29th, his team-mate Robinson, who had had the

179

distinction in 1958 of being the first British rider to win a stage, taking 26th place. Simpson almost won in the Paris-Roubaix (the biggest race of all except the Tour de France) and won the Tour de Flanders in 1961. He went on to win the classic Bordeaux-Paris, the 348 mile race for 'les grands', with a lead of 5min 4sec in 15hr 43min 47sec the next year. (It was the race which G. F. Mills, the great 'End-to-Ender', had won in its first year, 1891, in 26hr.) He achieved (in the Pyrenees) his yellow jersey or 'golden tunic' as a member of the Gitane team in the first trade team Tour de France for thirty-two years (1962), in which race he was never out of the first ten on general classification. Again in 1969 Barry Hoban of Calder Clarion CC won a stage. British riders were back on the continent!

The Tour de France ranks as one of the most brilliant sport shows in the world, as well as the roughest, toughest, most rewarding enterprise for competitors. Highly sophisticated organisation complements the super-fitness of the contestants; it is the tour that makes riders famous, not the riders that make the tour's fame. The accepted leader of a team is protected and supported by team-mates who will wait behind if he punctures, pace him back into position, hand over their bidons if he is thirsty, the contents of their musettes if he is hungry, and can be relied upon to 'look after' any too enterprising opposition; they act as *domestiques*, invaluable to any holder of the *maillot jaune* in his efforts to keep it. In the early stages of the tour, where there may be fifty or sixty riders in a sprint to finish at some sports stadium, their supporting tactics are quite half the battle. Continental teams have their *directeurs techniques*, who will order a move to attack, to drop back to help, or to come out of a break, and whose directive to the team may well be: 'you will all start the tour with equal rights until one of you proves himself worthy of exclusive protection. Then I will unite the rest of the team to work for him completely.' The *directeur* is not and cannot be associated with the cycle industry—

since in this race riders of different 'marques' and from various
trade teams are expected to combine forces in national interests.
Most *directeurs* have been riders themselves, know all the tricks
and enjoy the respect of their team : they are architects of victory.
The individual's main prop is the 'soigneur'—trainer, attendant,
masseur, adviser and nursemaid in more or less equal parts, without whose service the 'coureur' involved in continuous competition cannot expect to remain outstanding, however good he thinks
he is.

In the race itself it is usually one of the savage mountain stages—
if not the Pyrenees, then the Alps—that determines the eventual
winner. The Izoard, highest and steepest climb in the tour, drags
on and on right at the end of a gruelling day in the stage from
Gap to Brianon, and finally stamps FINISH on all those who are
not great stage riders.

> It presents a unique spectacle for hundreds of thousands of
> men, women and children who like to see the top riders romp
> away on its never-ending sides, and it stirs them to tears when
> they are forced to watch those who show their suffering more
> than others. They plod up over every painful inch, mouths
> wide open gasping for air, their faces, arms and legs per-
> manently covered in a glistening film of sweat.

The excitable French and Italians, who cross the border to cheer
on their favourites, cannot stop themselves giving a push here,
offering drinks or pouring ice-cold stream water over riders' heads.
'*Le peloton groupe*'—there are no breaks—may be the radio call
at the start, but not at the end. . . . Down then into the cold, shaded
plunge, the close sequence of hairpin bends, dark tunnels dripping
with water, grey-white glaciers hanging to the mountainsides—
braking, turning, then 'honking' away to maintain precious seconds'
advantage. Through towns and villages lined ten deep: flags,
flowers, paper-chains and banners everywhere—'Welcome to the
Tour.' The writer witnessed a small corner of a race of this type

L*

near the Mediterranean a year or two ago. Gendarmerie swarmed like bees, stopping and shepherding traffic off the main street. Police cars, ambulances, cars with spares stood by. There was a flurry of waving arms, flags, shrill blasts of whistles, sudden surges from the crowd, a last minute moving of cars with windscreens that flashed back the sun. Then a hush, a roar from down the line and the screaming sirens of motor-cycle outriders. The gendarmerie stood taut, stern, alert. The crowd tensed and, with a long drawn hiss of tyres, rush of air, whirl of spokes, rasp of labouring breath and flash of yellow, green, white and red jerseys, the peloton was round the bend, already past the corner. One name registered—G. Mariscotti and plaster on the owner's nose, knuckles and knees. Handbills fluttered from supporters' vans. The crowd sighed; the spectacle was over.

As has been said by Fausto Coppi, twice Tour de France winner, 1949 and 1952, Paris-Roubaix winner, five times Italian pursuit and four times Italian road champion, five times Giro d' Italia and Tour of Lombardy winner, World Hour Unpaced record holder, twice World Pursuit champion etc, the acknowledged *Campionissimo* : 'the mistake made by the youth of any country is that they are too eager to be world champions. They must look after themselves physically, they must learn the fibres of muscles and body; they must learn tactics, they must live, eat and dream road race.' Those 'tifosi'—the fans—and more serious sporting historians divide cycling into two parts: before Fausto Coppi and after Fausto Coppi. He was the first coureur to understand fully that racing is a technical and scientific job. His technique was such that he usually won on his own by minutes; second hands on the stop watch were rarely necessary, a photo-finish never, in his prime. The Frenchmen Anquetil (three times Tour de France winner) and Bobet, the Swiss Koblet and Kuhler, the Italian Magni, the Spaniard Poblet and others who followed Coppi, have acknowledged him as the greatest of all and risen to their world stature still in his shadow.

182

What, then, are the rewards for 'living, eating and dreaming road race', for the contestants in this and the major tours of Italy and Spain or in the eight road-racing classics—all of which have been won by one man only, the Belgian Van Looy? For some twenty cyclists perhaps not less than £10,000 a year; for a world star— say Eddy Merckx—whose sponsor's advertisement competes for place on his race clothing, up to or over £50,000; a share in team prizes, say £12-15,000 in a Tour de France. The winner's prize money is usually distributed among his team-mates who made his victory possible; his real emoluments, on a much enhanced scale, come from subsequent appearances as a 'star' among the *regionaux* at local races, and from contracts with organisers of criteriums. These shrewd businessmen give their home town or their firm's employees opportunity of seeing a race between riders who have made news in the Tour de France and reap the benefit of headlines again in the provincial press. The post-tour 'circus' forms the continental star's bread and butter : he no longer relies, as after World War I, almost entirely on earnings from the road classics. For British home-based professionals of perhaps ex-Olympic class a retainer of something like £1,500 a year can be doubled—by competing in as many as a hundred races.

At the time of writing the BCF is planning a conference for British organisers and promoters of professional races to discuss such questions as 'taking cycle racing to the public', and 'ensuring that a sponsor gets the publicity he needs', as well as 'promoting cycle racing for the benefit of riders'. Sponsors, it is recognised, generally come into the sport for one reason—it is cheaper than advertising on television or in the newspapers. But only with their fullest backing can British racing cyclists compete on level terms with the continental twelve-man trade teams and hope to hold their own in the increasingly sophisticated and expensive world of the major tours. Currently six sponsored clubs have been accredited out of the 700 in Britain.

At the same time UCI (Union Cyclists Internationale), the world body which wants to keep racing a tough sport, but not so hard as to induce riders to take artificial stimulants, has ruled that no professional race shall exceed a stage average of 200km (124½ miles) for twenty full racing days, with a maximum of 250km. So the current Tour de France has no longer the continuous line of a round-the-coast race, but includes 'hops' made by coach or train and airlifts between certain 'legs'. Simpson's death in the Tour de France, 1967, was a tragic lesson.

The Tour of Britain, which seems to gain most supporters, is not the only British road race although it is the outstanding stage race. The Tour of the North, a classic of the northern calendar, the Scottish 'Milk Race', the Irish Tour of the North, the Kermesse and international Mountain Time Trials held in the Isle of Man, the Criterium des Vainqueurs in Essex, the International Criterium at Southport, the Brighton Trophy Race, the Beaconsfield circuit Grand Prix—these are a few of the races offering first-rate spectator-rider participation in the spring and summer months, and rewards for both clubman and star. For hill-climb enthusiasts there is a national championship event held currently on the Horsehoe Pass, Llangollen, North Wales, in autumn.

Another, and typically British, form of event, the cyclo-cross race, has grown in the last twenty years into a winter sport attracting over a thousand participants. Its season lasts from November to February, its 'fields' are largest in the Birmingham and London areas, its organisation, the British Cyclo-Cross Association, was set up in 1954. For this combination of cycle-racing and cross-country running—or 'steeple-chasing' as it used to be in hunt parlance—held generally over an eight-mile course (sixteen for world champion titles), either as a time trial or as a massed-start race, success depends on the rider's robust fitness, strength and courage, and on a machine specially fitted to cope with mud.

'Yorkshire win team title in the snow : Cyclo Cross conquers

Big Freeze day for sport' are characteristic headlines, which tell
their own tale of conditions and the necessary competitors' quali-
ties. A cyclo-cross specialist, like John Atkins of Coventry RC, 'the
Sandhurst of cyclo-cross', winner of eight national championships
amateur and professional, or Paddy Hoban of the 'Nomads', an
international representative in world championship events, is prepared to cope with metal fences, flooded streams, railway sleepers,
farmyards, woodland tracks and oozing field paths, and race flat out
between. In the early days of the sport a 57in or 59in fixed gear
or a single-speed free was sufficient to win—a simple transmission
with nothing to choke with mud. Nowadays, faster and somewhat
more rideable courses have brought back gears; a high bottom
bracket, ample clearance at the frame's chainstays, forks and
bridges are means to avoid mud clogging, while light wired-on
tyres (instead of the sprinter's stuck-on type) and light alloy frame
and cranks cut weight down for a machine that has at times to be
carried and that may acquire four or five pounds of alluvium from
the course.

'You can get out of a bicycle in terms of speed only what your
own athletic ability enables you to put into it—which is what
makes cycle-racing a truly athletic sport.' In the opinion of physical
education experts 'the stage race cyclist is about the fittest sportsman in the world. His digestion is good—after all he eats while he
works—his recovery from exertion is remarkably quick, and he
uses his legs with extreme efficiency, *souplesse* as the French call
it.' The pleasure principle in the acquisition and use of *souplesse*
for its own sake is undoubtedly what excites most racing cyclists.
The silver and gold medals of the Olympics are there to provide
supreme standards. But today a member, say, of the Clitheroe section of the Clarion CC who adopts the profit principle can, if he
is extremely gifted and determined, climb into international status
almost as fast as a 'pop' star, and as a 'prince of pedallers' enjoy
almost as princely an income.

CHAPTER TEN

NEWER TYPES

THE FACT that most production bicycles manufactured up to and after World War I were of orthodox Safety design represents a truism of mechanical progress. A machine which had some 300 major components, or 1,500 minor ones, and whose construction involved the use of twenty or so different materials, needed, when it had reached satisfactory stability of evolution, to be built to a fairly constant pattern if advantage was to be taken of organised production techniques to keep down costs. On the one hand, having vast machinery already laid down for making bicycles (as a result of the vanished boom), manufacturers cannily went in for mass output of standardised articles—'One quality, one price, twelve guineas', as one old Coventry firm announced. The admission as late as 1926 by another world-famous Coventry firm that 'nearly all bicycle-makers have remained stagnant in the matter of bicycle design' was, in the long run, clearly suicidal. On the other hand, after the period of comparative standstill during the war and a marked decline in bicycle use after it as car and motorcycle exerted their still novel and powerful attractions, much attention was given to ways of improving design and reviving the market.

It was all very well, as J. B. Priestley noted in *Good Companions* (1929), for some people in those three Midland industrial towns, within a short non-stop run on the railway to either Manchester or Birmingham, that were 'known as the Triangle, and, more recently, since the towns gave themselves up to the mass production of cheap cars, the Tin Triangle'. All very well, 'when that daily procession of brand-new cars, shiny saloons or chassis with drivers perched on boxes slides away down the London Road, for such as J. J. Lumbden, the son of old Lumbden who kept the bicycle shop in Cobden Street [and] is worth nearly half a million and steadfastly refuses the most gigantic offer from America'. But for others still in the bicycle business in those places where every other man was a mechanic it was not nearly so well.

New designs were, broadly speaking, of two kinds: different forms and those resulting from different materials and/or methods of construction. The latter, in effect, led to the substitution of a new, lightweight type for the old, heavy 'gentleman's machine.' The frame had a shorter wheelbase, more upright steering-head, standard 26in instead of 28in wheels, tyres of 1¼in where they had been 1½in, lighter accessories and fittings. Subtle, carefully incorporated improvements and the use of both new welding, soldering and brazing methods and of new formula steels all contributed to a more compact, substantially lighter machine. As mentioned above, manganese-molybdenum and chrome-molybdenum steels, when they became available, made a big difference in weight-saving, while preserving or increasing strength where stress was greatest. Lighter alloys for parts under less stress, such as handlebars and pedals, and celluloid instead of metal for mudguards and chaincases, also made their contributions.

A traditional machine, the Rudge-Whitworth light roadster (1926), which included such requirements for touring as a 3-speed hub-gear, dependable brakes and sturdy section tyres, weighed 33lb in place of normal 'gentleman bicycle' weights of over 40lb. A lady's bicycle made by Swifts (1927) with reduced tyre section, and sprockets for altering the gear ratio, weighed 27lb. For track-racing machines in the late twenties the use of wooden rims, light 1in diameter tyres, duralumin parts and the lightest butted steel tubing made possible a weight of only 15lb.

> Observe the lady who has accepted the standard Roadster of the big maker, 1927 pattern. The handle-bar curls around her ears. The chain is covered with more obsolete relics of 1895 —either a Ford body in tin or an attaché-case of synthetic leather. These are 'to keep her skirt out of the chain', although that disappearing garment never comes within a foot of the chain. . . . The high wheels and bracket, the thick lifeless tyres are still those of 1895.

For the enlightened man or woman (and manufacturer), however,
> His bicycle is his third leg: and his other two being just about the same height, he can touch ground with both feet while seated. He has ten to fifteen pounds less weight, ten inches lower gear, two inches lower wheels, two inches lower crank-bracket, and two to four inches less frame height. He and his sister have found the Open Sesame to many of the best things life offers them. [Kuklos Papers, 1927]

Some firms had already 'folded' under economic difficulties and post-war pressures; for others amalgamation or absorption into larger concerns was a means of moving into the phase of trade revival, taking full advantage of large-scale mass-production methods. In 1932 the cycle interests of Humber Ltd were acquired by Raleighs—a process that was to be repeated in the next two decades until Raleighs owned Rudge-Whitworth, Triumph and BSA Cycles Ltd. During the thirties, after the Depression and the worst period of unemployment, a new bicycle sold for only £4—or four-pence weekly on hire purchase terms—and the highest-price de luxe models cost under £15. Following World War II prices at least doubled: a decent lightweight in 1960 cost £27.

Bicycling came in for notice again in the later twenties and the thirties.

> She'd a bicycle with a shopping basket
> And a harsh back-pedal brake

sang W. H. Auden in the ballad of Miss Gee; and, as tension mounted in the era of the Spanish Civil War and of Germany's open rearmament:

> Above them, expensive, shiny as a rich boy's bike,
> Aeroplanes drone through the new European air.
>
> [Dover]

As index of current public interest a poet's images and similes are not insignificant when they are focused as often as were Auden's at this time on bicycles—whether 'on the public ground fallen like huddled corpses', employed by Miss Gee to reach evening service or doctor's surgery, or in the more glamorous context of one 'applauding the circuits of racing cyclists'. Popular films also featured bicycles for exploiting the vivacity of their youthful heroines (as, in Edwardian days, was sometimes done in musical comedies, for the chorus), while in America bicycle parades were used to advertise the motion pictures featuring Deanna Durbin. (Bicycles also were central to the humour and social criticism of two distinguished post-war films, 'Jour de Fête' and the Italian 'Bicycle Thieves'.)

This interest was concomitant with health movements and the impetus given to outdoor activities by the formation of the Youth Hostels Association in 1930. Sunbathing as a 'cure-all', originally adopted in Germany to counter deficiency diseases in children during the post-war period of acute shortages, 'hiking', again developed from a German craze in the *wandervogel* era of Tyrolean costume, mandoline and *jugendherberger*, the availability of YHA beds in country places at one shilling per night—these helped to support the notion of simple life enjoyed in the open air already cherished by the cyclist. A distinctive dress—almost a uniform—became common wear for both walker and cyclist: open-necked khaki shirt, khaki shorts, Basque beret, short socks or khaki stockings. From the industrial towns one saw every weekend platoons, companies, battalions almost of similarly dressed young men and women streaming out of the smoke into the surrounding hills and dales—a sight much less common today. The present writer found himself 'in the movement'—with a rambling excursion through the Black Forest, cycling expeditions to the Scottish Isles and the west of Ireland. Party fares, low hostel charges and simple meals made possible then three weeks of cycling holiday abroad for about £15.

In the USA also bicycling enjoyed a come-back during the thirties—in spite of the powerful magnetism of other sports and means of transport. Well over a million machines were sold in 1937, appreciably more than in the previous peak year of 1899, although it was not so high a ratio on a population basis. In 1940 it was estimated that there was a ratio of one bicycle for every seventeen people (7 million machines in all), or one for every four automobiles. By 1950 production had gone up to 2 million, the output of fifteen major manufacturers, and altogether some 18 million were in use; by 1960 total sales were almost 3·5 million. Among the changes of design that helped to restore the American's interest in bicycles were better tyres, brakes, lights, suspension system and locking facilities. In the come-back period of the thirties there were about a hundred bicycle clubs in the USA and, corresponding to the CTC, the rather less flourishing League of American Wheelmen.

Correspondents to *The Times* deplored the 'spectacle of the country's youths and maidens in hideous uniforms', but the Bishop of Exeter showed that he was with the trend (1934), perambulating his diocese at the age of seventy-one on a bicycle of brilliant vermilion, and coming to the defence of hikers, most of whom had only one short holiday a year and were right to make it as interesting as possible and to enjoy it in the country. Stories by V. S. Pritchett revealed the wayside adventure-lure of cycling. Comic postcards featured the fate of the tandem pair with an oversize girl in ballooning khaki shorts at the front and the little man far too close behind to see the view: 'I've got a bit of grit in my eye, Bert!' 'Is that all, Lass ! You're LUCKY.'

Retrospectively, Professor Richard Hoggart saw in cycling's popularity in the thirties and after valuable evidence that urban working-class people could still react positively to both the challenge of their environment and the useful possibilities of cheap mass production . . .

> A sign of arrival at real adolescence is the agreement from one's parents to the buying of a bike on the hire-purchase system paid for out of weekly wages. Then one goes out on it at weekends, with a friend who bought a bike at the same time, or with one of those mixed clubs which sweep every Sunday through town and out past the quiet tram terminus.

Professor Hoggart went on to postulate the number of members of the two main cycling clubs (CTC and NCU) at a quarter of a million—a figure, however, which more than doubled the actual total of organised British cyclists in national, regional and local clubs.

The resurgence of interest in cycling, for the 'man in the street' as distinct from the specialist of road or track, was even more marked after the war. The need for economy during the recovery period, the lack of petrol for private use, the return of service men and women often aware of other countries, eager to enjoy freedom and to get about in the open both at home and on the continent, nostalgic memories, perhaps, of earlier, happier days, coupled with the attraction of the more efficient and pleasant improved lightweight bicycles on the market—all contributed to this trend. 'Me and My Bike' was the theme for a film operetta (unfinished) by Dylan Thomas. 'Keep a look out for us, we'll soon be coming your way' was a typical message on cards of this post-war period: they showed tanned and handsome bare-armed, bare-legged couples (man in front now), clearly out to enjoy their tandem riding. Country excursions and even extended touring trips with a small family became possible with the lighter tandem machine to which a light side-car could be added. The double gentlemen's model was now the type most favoured and, of course, increase of speed and double the propulsive drive went with much less than double the weight and friction. For the modern girl, in shorts or slacks, there was a choice of riding either in front or at the rear.

Different construction methods and materials account for much of trading progress in the second quarter of the twentieth century: but different forms also began to play their part, if only in indicating future possibilities. French ingenuity and publicity put a horizontal bicycle on the market in 1933. In this machine, the 'Velocar', a rider, lying on his back to lessen wind resistance, was able to employ both back and leg muscles to propel himself at speeds higher than could be achieved on the orthodox bicycle. Some world speed records were established with it and a touring model 'Velocar', incorporating a derailleur speed-gear and dynamo lighting-set, was produced. Too unconventional for the popular taste it nevertheless indicated one direction of the break-away from the diamond-frame convention. At the beginning of World War II an American firm, Whalen & Janssen (of Janssen Piano Company) developed a laminated wood-frame bicycle, to help in conserving critical materials. Fork, saddle, handlebars and elliptical frame were all of wood, but as this material later proved more 'critical' than metal, the type was not marketed. There were also experiments, French and English, for tourist use and for racing, with energy storage bicycles incorporating a fly-wheel addition. A novel-framed bicycle, intended by its designer to store energy by means of an electric device resembling a hub dynamo, was exhibited at the Festival of Britain, 1951. Neither scheme proved worthwhile for regular adoption.

Newer Types

In another direction there had already been exemplars, as long ago as 1886, with the 'level' cross-frame racer. With this form, in essence two long straight members joined at right angles, difficulties in achieving strength and stiffness tend to counter the advantages of simplicity and lightness. After World War II the aviation firm of Verdon-Roe produced an experimental cross-frame (1946) which, although it did not win general support, kept this alternative to the diamond frame under review. A few years later a German light-alloy cross-frame, made by die-casting process, proved the means of building a touring bicycle that weighed only 25lb. In Italy, well before the war, the 'Velocino' had established a certain popularity for use in town and on short runs, with its greatly reduced front wheel and length of wheelbase, which made it both lighter and more compact than such traditional machines as the Bianchi. The makers also claimed in its favour greater comfort and safety.

THE SMALL REVOLUTION

The bicycle that combined both main features, cross-frame and small wheels, was introduced in Britain by Alex Moulton in 1962. It had 16in diameter wheels, oval-section tubes, and a special rubber suspension system. After certain difficulties had been overcome at stress points in the frame and the novelty of its toy scooterish look had been accepted, the Moulton bicycle became an outstanding success. So much so that it was welcomed as a revolutionary design and went far to revitalise the whole industry, which was contracting again in the latter half of the 1950s when increased affluence at home gave to the bicycle a socially inferior 'image' (perceptible in John Wain's novel 'Hurry on Down') and low-cost competition from eastern European countries and Japan closed large export markets.

The Hulton Readership Survey, 1952-5, suggested that there had been a slight drop in the popularity of cycling 'during the last few years'. The most common users were men in the socio-economic group termed 'working-class' and 'poor'—40 per cent of all users (the two groups together comprised 71 per cent of all informants); women in those groups used cycles slightly less than the women in the other classes, ie the lower middle class, middle and well-to-do. The finding was, perhaps, no more remarkable than that arrived at some fifteen years later in a market research sample survey of British tastes that, 'in the absence of cars, mopeds and bicycles are most popular in East Anglia, the flat lands being happily suited to the latter.' (East Anglia has been the breeding ground of not a few fine racing cyclists.) In Scotland the same survey found that 'the Highland zone because of its much greater hilliness discourages bicycle ownership quite drastically', whereas, in the cities, 'flat or tenement living greatly reduces the number of cycles, scooters and mopeds'.

An indication of the industry's need of some such lift as that given by the Moulton is afforded by the 'I think I'll buy a bicycle' theme adopted for 1958. The British Cycle Industries Association welcomed the co-operation of *Tit-Bits* in running a 'Why-to-Buy-a-Bike' competition in which bicycles were given as prizes. Entrants had to put in order the ten best reasons for buying a bicycle out of the following: affords healthy and enjoyable open-air exercise; little or no maintenance costs; useful for shopping; very modest purchase price; enables one to enjoy social life offered by cycling clubs; cuts travel costs to small fraction; takes up little space at home; highly manoeuvrable in traffic; solves the get-to-work problem; cheap and simple to transport by plane, train or ship; easy hire-purchase facilities; learning to ride safely is simple and quick; gives easy access to countryside; easily 'parked' when out shopping or visiting; dealers everywhere offer after-sales service . . .

At a Bicycle Industries Convention of the same year there was also circulated—for its propaganda value in the advocacy of cycling—an article summarising the findings of Dutch, German and Scandinavian medical authorities on the use of bicycles among school children, miners threatened by silicosis and convalescent TB patients. One and all found it positively beneficial, largely because it compels the rider to practise deep and rhythmical respiration. American authorities also recommend bicycling for children with weak bone structure and continue to use the bicycle for physiological investigations into circulatory function.

Moulton's name had been made with the hydrolastic car suspension that helped the 'Mini' to capture world markets. His suspension technique applied to personal transport made possible smoother and easier riding—added manoeuvrability and less tyre friction—with hard-pumped tyres. The system was two-fold and unique, in design. Current models have in front a coil spring with special rubber dampening, with return compensation operating on a serrated guide tube, the exposed area being protected by a rubber bellows. This 'irons out the bumps'. Rear suspension incorporates an independent rear fork pivoting immediately behind the bottom bracket, and a special metal-bonded-to-rubber unit, for springing and shock absorbing, working in sheer and compression to give greater dampening effect (Major de Luxe). The Mark III has in the rear a 'squash ball' shock absorber—also unique of its kind. The result, with a frame 'customised' to fit anyone is a smooth stable ride. The Moulton is the only small wheel cycle that has proved itself able with the modification of narrower rims and tyres to approach the performance of the orthodox cycle, in racing. Moreover, one has been ridden from England to Australia.

The revolutionary Moulton design led to many variations on the same theme, such as the Raleigh small wheel (16in) of 1965, which was eventually to outsell its progenitor. When, in August 1967, the business of Moulton bicycles was amalgamated with Raleigh—who by this time had acquired Carlton Cycles, racing model and sports specialists, Phillips, Hercules, Sun, and Norman among others

two most dynamic forces in the whole industry were brought together. Raleigh claim to be the world's largest producers of personal
two-wheeled transport, with 70 per cent of total cycle production,
75 per cent of their output going to markets overseas.

With new dynamic sales promotion a new image was created.
'The quickest way to the fun scene is by bicycle. Small-wheel to be
right in the trend. Swingers love their go-anywhere features—like
the finger-tip seat and handlebar adjustment—and the big, big hold-
alls that let you carry everything for fun.' With revised versions
such as the Triumph Twenty (20in) 'Shopper' for housewives, the
Sun 'Sporting 20', and the RSW 14 for 'Tweeny Boppers', the
bicycle became 'with it' once again. The accent was on style, easy
handling, colourful appearance and, a thoughtful point in town,
freedom from traffic 'snarl-ups'. Later 'marks' had twist-grip gear
controls as well as quick-release levers for handlebar and saddle
positions. A characteristic note in publicity was to photograph a
machine in, say, tropic blue enamel with white-wall tyres before
the matching white and blue porch of a superior middle-class
house, alongside the equally smart family car; or to display it in
the grounds of a classy preparatory school, outside a 'trendy'
boutique or coiffeur's. The intended deductions are obvious. 'New
Look models for teenagers and adults' (slogans of Coventry Eagle)
summed up the marketing approach. The small wheel and the mini-
skirt fashion happily coincided. The revitalised trade in Britain,
after the period of the fifties when Raleigh output fell by 50 per
cent, forms part of the picture of a general advance. From 1958 to
1970 the estimates of bicycles in use throughout the world moved
up from 100 million to well over 150 million.

The full specification of a Raleigh Moulton Mark III—the
'sophisticated GT bicycle for the 1970s'—is as follows:

FRAME   Open type: designed to suit everyone from
                          8/9 year-olds to adults of 6ft and over.

WHEELS   Rustless spokes: Dunlop high-pressure tyres,
                          $16 \times 1\frac{3}{8}$.

GEARS	Twist-grip control sets pace of the Sturmey-Archer gear.
HANDLEBARS	All-rounder style. Finger-formed black vinyl grips.
LIGHTING	Plain bracket for front and rear lights.
MUDGUARDS	Smart, plain and narrow guards. Reflector on rear.
PEDALS	Bow type: black rubbers. Individual amber reflectors.
BRAKES	Caliper front, hub rear with black cables.
SADDLE	Black cover. Seat pillar adjusts to height required via quick-release lever.
REAR CARRIER	Big capacity for shopping and usual household loads.
SUSPENSION	Revolutionary front and rear. Assures the most comfortable of rides.
FINISH	Choice of White/Satin Black, Tropic Blue/Satin Black or Royal Carmine/Satin Black.
PRICE	£37 including purchase tax.
OPTIONAL EXTRA	£2 19s 3d for holdall.

'Who'd have thought anything as utilitarian as a bicycle could be downright elegant—a devastatingly good-looking gad-about that'll have everyone's head turning. It's a machine designed for switched-on people of any age: as smart as tomorrow.' So of the RSW Mark III with its gracefully curved Y-shaped handlebars and tartan-finish holdall. Another variant of the 'bicycle isn't just a plaything' theme came from an Austrian firm, Steyr-Daimler-Puch, whose British base is in Nottingham. Their 'Camping 20' model takes apart into four easily stowable sections, which can be stored in a car boot and reassembled in thirty seconds for riding. The same firm also produce a 'Cantilever' economy model for boys and girls, with curved top and bottom tubes and a curved extension to the seat stay crossing between them, bearing some slight resemblance to Starley's original 'Rover' safety, less to the Dursley-Pedersen cantilever.

197

Newer Types

Latest type from Raleigh, introduced in the North American market in 1969, is the 'Chopper', a 'real scorcher for girls and boys from 8-14'. Its high-back polo-type saddle, chrome roll-bar for 'fast back' look, stick-shift gear control, coil-spring shock absorbers, speed indicator panel, high-rise handlebars, twin-boom crossbar, kick-into-position prop-stand and large diameter heavy-tread tyres make it look as much as possible like something else. How its particular image accords with the National Safe Cycling scheme for children (originally inspired by R. C. Shaw, MBE, secretary of the CTC) and the efforts of the Royal Society for the Prevention of Accidents, or can help to promote good cycle riding, is a moot point. The craze, however, for 'Easy Rider' styles has swept Europe. The German *Kinder* model, 'Kettrad Pirate', currently sells at £21.80 as compared with the Raleigh at £35 (including 30 per cent purchase tax). The British 'Chopper', introduced in June 1970, has constructional superiority, but the Kettrad has its dynamo set, saddle rack, parcel clip and superior paint finish. Its low price is partly due to the size of the domestic market, plus the fact that fourteen-year-olds in Germany are permitted to ride 25cc mini-motor bikes, costing as little as £35, which tends to keep down pedal bicycle prices.

As Raleighs emphasise, the wedge-frame 'Chopper' is 'a machine that's got the sort of power and dash normally encountered only on the circuit: a machine inspired by the screaming rubber and roaring fantails of the dragster racing slick'. It is designed on 'taut, tearaway-and-love-it lines'; not surprisingly, its 750cc motorised equivalent rates a prominent place among contemporary 'pop' posters. But for this 'bike with burn-up potential' there are at any rate some safety considerations in the form of caliper brakes, a large back reflector and additional pedal reflectors, while the speed indicator panel actually indicates the Sturmey-Archer 3-speed gear changes. For the 'high-rise' or 'apehanger' handlebars there was in British manufacture an early precedent. A fairly early 'Safety' with just such handlebar shape was included in the Bartleet Bicycle

Newer Types

Collection, labelled simply—'a freak'. . .

This 'most successful single bicycle ever produced' received immediate acclaim in the USA where everybody owned a car and the bicycle as means of transport had come to be regarded as a toy. Up to the sixties youth was the marketing target. Production concentrated on clumsy gimmicks, girder front forks, long wide handlebars, balloon tyres, even sometimes a dummy petrol tank to match the appearance of a motor-cycle. A too casual attitude to safety factors and the belief in planned obsolescence has militated against American makes. A Consumers' Union survey found, even before World War II, that with one or two exceptions foreign bicycles excelled American products in point of serviceability. English, French, German, Dutch and Italian led the field. There is evidence still in American magazine publicity given to such machines as 'a custom-built English ten-speed model tandem weighing a scant 44 pounds' (*Playboy*, August 1971), that the cognoscenti look elsewhere than to the home product. In bicycles Americans tend to *buy* British and *sell* overseas. There is, of course, Raleigh Industries (of America) Inc at Boston, Massachusetts, as a major source of supply. Import of Japanese 'run-about' models and of continental components, such as Huret derailleur gears, also diversify the market in which such firms as Harris D. P. Hardware & Manufacturing Co, New York and the American Machine and Foundry Co, Madison Avenue, New York are home producers.

Today, however, genuine enthusiasm for cycling as a hobby—partly as a revolt against an over-mechanised age—exists in America. Youth hostels (the American movement began in 1934) and sponsored tours have long had their select following. Some enthusiasts see in Europe—or saw pre-war, while the bicycle there corresponded to an automobile in USA—'a paradise of the bicyclist'. The new resurgence of interest (chiefly among adults concerned with keeping or getting in better physical condition) is currently putting Central Park, New York, at the hub of the

199

American cycling scene. Since the park has been closed to motor traffic at weekends and on certain weekday evenings, some ten thousand cyclists young and old, make the circuit (a six and a half mile lap) or foregather there simply to 'talk bikes' and admire their mechanics, in the course of a day. Prestige models cost up to $375. 'Pedal power—for carefree relaxation and pollution-free transportation' is one side of it; the other is the chance this activity affords to break through age, income, race and status barriers and enjoy contacts in the community of sport. Sales, again, have mounted sharply in the last decade . . .

In this context it is the 'neighbourhood role' rather than the wider travel or exploratory use that seems likely to underwrite the bicycle's future. Town planners are accommodating and encouraging the idea. In Droitwich, twenty miles south of Birmingham, for example, apart from a new road pattern to take heavy fast traffic and an independent pattern to link residential areas and industrial estates, it is currently proposed that a separate pattern of pedestrian and cycle routes be developed. These would link schools, shops, places of employment and the countryside to the homes. The pattern would develop from the existing footpaths radiating from the fringes of the town to rural areas and extend through both new and existing urban areas. In other areas children going to school, women shopping or making local calls, fathers providing a 10-speed sports model (however unsuitably) to a ten-year-old youngster to impress his pals, or themselves 'hacking' to work for fitness' sake—these make good sale losses in other directions.

In America bicycles are at present 'big business' and there is something in the nature of a boom. Amateur cycle racing clubs have felt the resurgence; growing numbers commute to work by bicycle; there is a movement to establish cycle lanes in city streets, including Fifth Avenue, Seattle and San Francisco. Medical journals stress the bicycle's rôle as a peaceful, easy-going contributor to health, and even as a factor in population control. 'The infertility of a husband was traced to his habit of riding his bicycle to work and back for about two and a half hours every day; when he ceased to ride for a while his wife became pregnant.' (*Pharmaceutical Journal*, October 1971). Bicycling as therapy for recovered drug addicts is another current notion. But like so many crazes —and in this one the swing over in sales of adult machines has been from 20 per cent to 65 per cent of total sales within the last five years—bicycling may fade in favour of something else. There remains, as main support to the industry, whatever happens in over-developed countries, a great demand for bicycles in the under-developed countries.

In serious cycling circles in Britain the general tenor of comment is upon the continually shrinking numbers of competition entrants and of affiliations to the national body. Whereas in France licence holders have increased by almost 8,000 in the last decade to a total of 47,000, in Britain the BCU has recorded a drop of almost twenty per cent in members during that decade's second half, bringing down the total to just over 8,000. Teams and individuals are beset by the problem of lack of funds adequate to put them on terms of competitive parity with continentals in the big international events. Racing promoters must 'go to the public', or ambitious riders must go to the continent, whether for edge or backing or both. The CTC admirably serves national and local interests, from Godalming, its headquarters now, and embraces cycling and social activities in two hundred local groups. But each £2 subscription seems a fraction less certain than it did the year before, as membership hovers around 20,000. If a current proposal to make cyclists carry third party insurance were to become law, what its effects would be on this trend can scarcely be in doubt.

The journal which first appeared in 1891 as *Cycling* appears today as *Cycling and Mopeds*. Every issue has its features on maintenance, road tests, fuel consumption, handling (for beginners) and

201

M

the comparative performance of various British and continental makes of machine in which pedals are present merely as a subsidiary. 'Powered cycling' has acquired modish appeal, but as an idea it is nearly as old as the hobbyhorse itself. A cartoon of a steam-driven velocipede, a hobbyhorse of the period with an embryonic steam engine at the rear, appeared in France in 1818. Caricatures by John Leech, at the end of the hobbyhorse era, projected similar notions of two- or three-wheeled steam traction without, of course, indicating technical means.

The practical beginning of the application of engine assistance to the bicycle belongs to the Michaux era. In 1869 a compact steam engine unit, of Perraux origin, was fitted under the saddle and operated the rear wheel of a Michaux velocipede by a leather driving belt—thus providing the prototype for both the powered cycle and the motor-cycle proper. Various other applications of steam power to tricycles and bicycles were tried out in Britain and in America in the late 1870s and the 1880s, before the simultaneous appearance of the Safety bicycle and the internal combustion engine about 1885 made possible the later commercial production of motorised bicycles.

The resultant machine, when it appeared about the turn of the century, took one of two general forms: a standard safety bicycle, unaltered structurally, with a self-contained engine attachment; or a machine with strengthened forks and offset rear wheel, induction system in the steering-head and engine attached thereto, the ancestor of the motor-cycle. The former, incorporating a cyclemotor unit, has its own history, too complex for inclusion here, with periods of popularity before World War I and after World War II both for British-made and for continental machines. The Singer 'motor-wheel', dating from 1900, a self-contained replacement for either front or rear wheel of a bicycle, was also important for a type which came into its own fifty years later.

The cyclemotor in the beginning was regarded as a means of

helping the cyclist to pedal against head-winds or up long hills. While petrol was cheap between the wars and small cars were becoming widely popular, less attention was given to the motor-assisted bicycle in Britain than on the continent, where new German and Italian designs supplied a steadily increasing demand. After World War II the need for economy, both in petrol and in expenditure, brought this form of cheap mechanical transport into more general use. 'Clip-on units'—placed under the pedal bracket and driving the rear wheel by a friction wheel—and self-contained motorised wheels were probably the most favoured types of power assistance; the unit mounted on the front down tube of the diamond frame, or on the steering-head to drive the front wheel by friction collar (like the early 'Ixion', 1903, and the Berini M13 of the fifties) had some clear advantages but less appeal. With the progress already noted in the use of materials and techniques of manufacture, the additional weight need only be in the order of from 15lb to 25lb instead of 40lb; speeds of up to 30mph with fuel consumption as little as 300mpg could be obtained in place of the normal 18mph and 160mpg with former units. Singer's 'Cyclemaster', BSA's 'Winged Wheel', Hercules' rotary-engine unit, were popular British examples of the motorised wheel, while the Trojan mini-motor unit, fixed over the rear wheel, operated by friction wheel. The bicycle itself from 1950 onwards was likely to have a specially strengthened frame and sprung front forks.

'Our family is mad about Mopeds. . . . Hand-operated front and rear brakes, a twist-grip throttle and a simple trigger clutch to free the drive from the single gear. These were all I had to worry about. I had but to pedal away, open the throttle, drop the clutch and there I should be, power-propelled. This, I thought, is going to be easy.' So, in 1957, the housewife who had dropped ordinary cycling for family chores, is encouraged to take it up again in its new form. After a morning's practice on the lawn and in nearby lanes, she finds her cycle-bred road sense returns, is still perfectly fresh and is amazed by the complete sense of security that the novice feels from the outset on these 'fascinating machines'....

So the whole family can be on wheels with minimum pedal effort (only up the steepest hills) and without the disparity in energy making a joint outing burdensome to either old or young. A child or an elderly person can ride it. With such refinements as automatic gear, adapting itself to prevailing conditions of road and load, 'fusslessness' of hill climb, reliable cruising speed of 25-30mph, stream-lined frame and front and rear suspension, the 'Cyclemate', the Dutch two-seater 'Centro', the Italian Cucciolo and Lambretta, the French Motorbecane 'Mobymatic', the German Heinkel and NSU 'Quickly', the Norman 'Nippy' (British with German engine), the Raleigh 'Moped' and their contemporaries and successors went far to meet the average British family man's dream in the 'You've-never-had-it-so-good' era. London to the Highlands and back with luggage for two for fifty shillings!

Purists, of whom the cycling movement has nourished not a few, regarded these things sadly or cynically. Rumney, whose cycling career extended to the end of the twenties, tried the early 'auto-wheel', but found the noise very uncomfortable and missed the delight of free-wheeling down the slopes as the engine slowed him. although the ability to surmount stiff hills without 'horse labour' was an admitted improvement. Finally, he abandoned both 'auto-wheel' and the motor-cycle with which he had a brief flirtation, and never resumed either. As for the car, he remarks how much more vivid was his recollection of a Highland tour which he had made formerly by bicycle than that after a quite recent motor tour of the same district, attributing this to the too rapid succession of scenes which flit by the motor vehicle. His attitude was that the modern cycle, with gears to suit the rider's locality and his years, cancelled the burden of age and restored both immediacy of enjoyment and all the vividness of later impression. In his time, among Safeties only, he had a Rover, two Dursley-Pedersens, a Raleigh,

Newer Types

New Rapid, Rudge, James, Endrick (with French 4-speed gear), Sunbeam, Humber, Centaur, BSA, and a light-weight Evans with Chemineau derailleur 3-speed (78, 62 and 44). He found that the modern cycle with modern road surface more than counterbalanced the addition of his age and carried him still easily up every hill on his well-known beat from London to Keswick in Cumberland.

Mopeds were departing from the main principle on which the bicycle had for so long held its own.

It is the vehicle on which the world rides for convenience and pleasure wherever roads run. It is far better to be personally independent in the matter of travel by ownership of a bicycle, than to rely on the far more expensive and complicated means which, at the end, have only bought speed. In the process they may have lost you the health, the activity, the silence and the delight that is wedded to personal travel in the cycling sense of that term.

The writer subscribes to that view, given reasonable road conditions, after cycling experience in places as far apart as Kyleakin and Kathmandu. In a space age increasingly subject to the threats of noise, excessive speed, and pollution, there is still a significant place for the balanced wheel.

SELECT BIBLIOGRAPHY

Books:

Anon. *Bicycling: A Textbook for Early Riders.* 1874

Bartleet, H. W. *Bartleet's Bicycle Book.* 1931

Bidlake, F. T. *Cycling.* 1896

Bowden, K. and Matthews, J. *Cycle Racing.* 1965

Bury, Viscount and Hillier, Lacy. *Cycling* (Badminton Library of Sport). 1887

Catalog of the Cycle Collection of the Division of Engineering. *United States National Museum.* 1953

Caunter, C. F. *Cycles—History and Development.* 1955

C.T.C. British Road Book. 1893

Fraser, Foster. *Round the World on a Wheel* (in 1896). 1925

Geist, R. C. *Bicycling as a Hobby.* 1940

Griffin, H. H. *Cycles and Cycling.* 1890

Henderson, N. G. *Continental Cycle Racing.* 1971

Hinxman, S. *Fifty Years of Road Riding.* 1935

Jerome, J. K. *Three Men on the Bummel.* 1900

'Kuklos' (Fitzwater Wray). *Across France in Wartime.* 1916

The Kuklos Papers. 1927

Lightwood, J. T. *The C.T.C.* 1928

Messenger, Charles. *Conquer the World*

Moxam, S. H. *Fifty Years of Road Riding.* 1935
Pemberton, A. C. *Cycling.* 1896
Pratt, Charles. *The American Bicycler.* 1879
Robinson, B. Fletcher (ed). *The Complete Cyclist.* 1897
Rumney, A. W. *Cyclist Touring Guides.* 1900-1
               Fifty Years a Cyclist. 1928
Shipway, H. S. *Post Office Cycles* (Green Paper 22). n.d.
Southcott, E. J. (ed). *First Fifty Years of Catford C.C.* 1939
Spencer, Charles. *The Bicycle—its Use and Action.* 1870
               The Bicycle Roadbook. 1881
Stevens, T. *Around the World on a Bicycle.* 1887
Sturmey, H. *The Indispensable Bicyclist's Handbook.* 1879
Trapmann, A. H. *The Military Cyclist's Vade Mecum.* 1909
Wells, H. G. *The Wheels of Chance.* 1898
Wood, J. L. *Cycles: a Short History.* 1970

      Periodicals:
Coureur
Cycling
Cycling Life (Chicago)
C.T.C. Gazette
International Cycle Sport
Le Velo
The Bicycle
The Boneshaker
The Cyclist
The Golden Penny
The Mechanic's Magazine
Wheeling

INDEX

Index

Index

213

Index